Help During Loss

A Guide to Recovery

Help During Loss

A Guide to Recovery

J. Mark and Kathy Ammerman

WINEPRESS **WP** PUBLISHING

Printed in the United States of America

Packaged by WinePress Publishing, PO Box 428, Enumclaw, WA 98022. The views expressed or implied in this work do not necessarily reflect those of WinePress Publishing. Ultimate design, content, and editorial accuracy of this work are the responsibilities of the authors.

Unless other wise noted all scriptures are taken from the Holy Bible, New King James Version, Copyright © 1979, 1980, 1982 by Thomas Nelson, Inc., Publishers. Used by permission.

ISBN 1-57921-220-4
Library of Congress Catalog Card Number: 99-62977

With sincere appreciation to
Jeanne Chirico
&
Pat Heffernan
of
Genesee Region Home Care
(Hospice)
for giving us the opportunity
to learn more about
and work with those in grief

Contents

Introduction

In our book *Help During Grief*, we explored the despair of losing a loved one. It is a despair which we both personally experienced. It is best understood if you realize that it throws you into a cycle that you don't want, didn't ask for, and will hate to experience. It is a process that we found must be completed in order to move on to a healthy lifestyle once again. Understanding the phases of this cycle benefits the bereaved person because it can help him or her know what to expect.

We have revised and expanded *Help During Grief*, and retitled it *Help During Loss*, because it contains added information that we have learned during the past few years. For example, we still see the grief cycle as being divided into parts, but we now label these as *phases* instead of *stages*, because they blend into each other much of the time.

Help During Loss is more than just information about the grief cycle. It is also about hopelessness, and explores reasons why these hopeless feelings persist for such a long time. It offers coping strategies that have proved helpful to us and the bereaved people we now work with through Hospice. We explore the hurtful experience of grief that sets the survivor apart from others. We discuss the new understanding that a bereaved person gains about the final stage in this world: death and its aftermath.

The emotional suffering caused by the death of a loved one contaminates the entire soul. It contaminates the way you think and process data. It contaminates the emotions. They are in chaos and make no sense. It also contaminates the will so that it cannot function properly. You will for things to return to normal, but that is now impossible. It is equally impossible to accept the reality of the situation at first.

Grief seems to change the entire personality. Actually, it simply may bring forth traits that the person always possessed but never had to use before. The innocence that was previously there is gone, and it will never be restored. It has been tainted with an ugly truth. As adults, we do not think of ourselves as still possessing innocence, but we do until we have experienced the death of a loved one.

If you are in grief, you will surely recognize yourself in these pages. You will see that others, in their own way, have been where you find yourself right now. If, on the other hand, you are a friend of someone in grief, then by reading *Help During Loss* you will find that you're better equipped to understand what hopelessness means. You will also understand that there is nothing you can do to "make it better."

If you have not experienced grief, be thankful. If you have, we hope you find comfort in this book.

If tears could build a stairway
And memories were a lane,
I would walk all the way to Heaven
to bring you home again.

No farewell words were spoken
No time to say good-bye,
you were gone before I knew it
and only God knows why.

My heart still aches in sadness
and secret tears still flow,
what it meant to lose you
no one will ever know...

Shirley Doyle

The Grief Cycle
&
Recovery

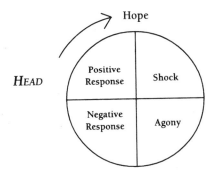

HEAD

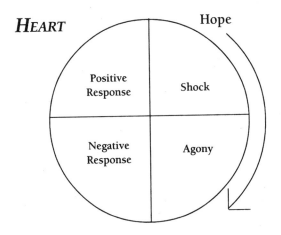

HEART

1

The Grief Cycle Explained

I n every person, grief follows a general pattern. Yet each person's grief is unique, in that each will follow this pattern in a different way. You can easily understand the grief cycle if you visualize both a large and a small circle (see previous diagram). We refer to these circles as the clocks of grief. The small circle/clock is in your head, while the larger circle/clock is in your heart. Each clock is divided into four phases. The first phase is shock, the second is agony, the third is negative response, and the fourth is positive response.

Bereaved people must complete this cycle so they can begin living healthy lives once again. Understanding the process can help to expedite it. The length of time it takes you to complete it will be determined by a variety of factors: your support system, your faith in God, your overall personality, and the circumstances surrounding the death.

The first phase of the grief cycle is shock. This phase comes into play when you're confronted with the news of the death. You don't believe what you're being told. Your loved one cannot be dead; you won't accept this information. You believe that this situation is *not* going to continue, that everything will return to normal. You are trying to compute the truth of what you're hearing, but your mind does so only a little at a time.

The second phase of the cycle—agony—brings with it a sense of isolation and heaviness. It is the ripping away of innocence that can never be restored. This is where the deep hurtful feelings are sinking in. Only those who have been there can truly understand this phase. The pain during the agony phase goes deeper than can possibly be described, and it will certainly last longer than you would ever believe.

The third phase, the negative response, is where the anger or, in some cases, the depression (which is just anger without energy) toward the situation appears. Several negative behaviors are often associated with this phase: suicidal thoughts, drug or alcohol use, possible promiscuity, or other behavioral changes. All these behaviors are really just attempts to ease the pain. The negative response phase *must* be exposed and dealt with in order to move into the fourth phase.

The fourth phase is the positive response. As you first enter the grief cycle, this is the phase that seems the least possible to experience. You cannot imagine ever having hope again or daring to go on without your loved one. But you can sense that you're in this phase when you get glimmers of hope. You might go out for an evening with a friend, come home, and briefly think about what a nice time you had. Overwhelming guilt might quickly follow this thought. You may find yourself wondering, *How could I even conceive of having a good time without...?* Gradually, this positive response phase will come into play more and more, and the guilt that may accompany it will abate.

The small clock in your head will speed through the cycle in a relatively short time, but down in your heart the larger clock is turning much more slowly. An added complication is that you won't go through this cycle in any logical order. In the morning, you might be feeling pretty good (the positive response phase) but by early afternoon you might find you're feeling quite angry (the negative response phase), then by evening you might be feeling completely hopeless about the future (the agony phase).

It is a very confusing time, and you need to be honest about where you are in the cycle—both with yourself and with those who are emotionally supporting you. If you know where you are, you will be better able to cope and to get help from others.

There is a third circle in the grief cycle in addition to the clocks in your head and heart. This is the circle of hope, which encompasses the other two. We are all born with hope—but when we experience grief, our hope may be nothing more than a small flicker. As we successfully move through the phases of the grief cycle, the hope becomes increasingly evident, until finally, in the midst of the positive response phase, we can see it clearly, although just briefly at first. As we continue in the positive response phase, the hope keeps growing.

The grief process is the only way for us to deal with loss. If this process is aborted, or happens too quickly, we end up in an atmosphere of emotional dishonesty. This can lead to suppressed anger and resentment which can have both mental and physical effects.

Therese Rando writes in *How to Go On Living When Someone You Love Dies* that your grief will take longer than most people think. It will take an unbelievable amount of strength. It will impact all spheres of your life. You will find yourself grieving for many things that are encompassed by the death. The loss may resurrect old issues, feelings, and unresolved conflicts from the past. You may experience grief spasms which are acute upsurges of grief that occur suddenly and without warning.

One of the most important points Rando makes is about the intensity of the grief. It will not only be more intense than you expected, but it will also become apparent in ways that you may not have anticipated. Aspects of your personality might emerge that you did not know were there. These seemingly new personality traits might assert themselves now to assist you in coping with these also-new intense emotions.

2

Mark's Story

Kathy and I met over the telephone one night. Her husband, Jerry, had died of a heart attack just a few weeks before, and she had reached her lowest point. She was contemplating suicide, but, at the urging of a friend, had called me for some advice. She wanted to know if I would come and talk with her. I did, and a few months later while we were at dinner together, I realized that this woman was a total surprise to me.

I felt stirrings of hope, and had an excited but cautious premonition that this particular woman might end the six lonely years of dreary limbo that I had been in since my wife was killed. My father, a chaplain and counselor, didn't hesitate to tell me that I had failed to act professionally because I allowed emotions to enter into a relationship with a counselee. However, since this led to marriage, he blessed me anyway.

In a different life, which had ended six years before, I was married to my first wife, Sherry. With our two daughters, Rebekah and Elisabeth, we were the quintessential pastor's family. We diligently worked at our faith and collectively were growing in God. We were fundamental, Spirit-filled Christians. I pastored the church and Sherry led our Christian school as principal.

We also had an unusual outreach ministry—bikers, primarily the Hell's Angels on the East Coast. That was why this particular night, the night Sherry died, found us on my Harley-Davidson Wideglide. We had ridden into the city to continue our ministry to bikers and dancers. It had been a successful night. Sherry had been able to pray with a dancer, and we both were happy and excited with what we saw happening.

It started raining on the way home. I remember thinking the rain would damage Sherry's new suede coat. The last few miles were foggy and wet so we were riding at a very moderate speed, enabling us to talk about the events of the night. As I stopped for the last traffic light, Sherry said, "I'm glad you're driving this big machine." Those would be her final words to me. We then started down the straight stretch of dark country road toward home. Suddenly, the bike hydroplaned. I knew we were going down. I remember thinking, *I'm sliding a long way,* and then putting my hands down to try to stop myself.

When I finally managed to come to a skidding halt, I sat stupefied on the side of the road. I began to call out for Sherry, but there was no answer. *This is going to upset her,* I thought. I continued to shout her name and began to search for her. It was so dark and foggy. I couldn't see anything. The bike had landed in a ditch, so I couldn't even use the headlights to help me in my search. I continued shouting her name while running up and down the long stretch of road, searching frantically, so afraid a truck would come by and run her over.

I searched for just over an hour, exhausted, scared, and frustrated beyond reason, when a truck finally did come by. I flagged it down. With the driver's help, I at last found Sherry. She was beyond where the bike had landed, not in back of it where, in my stunned condition, I assumed that she must be. No wonder I hadn't found her!

Having been a Kansas City police officer for seven years, I had seen plenty of fatalities, and seeing the way Sherry was folded in half, I knew she was dead. I unfolded her and watched as her head rolled like a rag doll's. Her neck had been broken in the crash, and she had died instantly. As I sat cradling her in my arms, the truck driver went for help.

I started talking to her like I always did, only she wouldn't respond. A part of me knew with certainty that she was indeed dead, but the rest of me would not, could not, accept or tolerate that fact. I began claiming all the faith verses I could recall, shouting commands for her to come back to life. I pleaded with God, "With both our faiths, it's possible, with the agreement of two or more where God is in the midst...Sherry, help, tell Him you want to come back. Our ministry isn't finished. It has always been us to-gether. We *have* to be together!!"

The policeman would not tell me she was dead. He was going to let the doctor do that. I was just sitting in the po-lice car, detached from the reality of the situation. The am-bulance crew was working on her in the ditch. I knew their efforts were futile, but even with this knowledge I refused to accept the truth. They took her to the hospital in the ambulance; I followed in the police car.

It felt like everybody in the emergency room was star-ing at me. The doctor asked me to come into his office. I could see Sherry's feet under the sheet. He told me he had done all he could and he was very sorry. He asked if I wanted some time with her.

As I stood alone with Sherry, I gazed down at her and said, "Sherry, don't do this to us. What am I going to tell our daughters? They're too young at only 13 and 10 to cope with this. They're home sleeping on the front porch. You're so full of life, everybody says so. This just can't be. You believe the Scriptures about having the right to live three-score and ten years. What about the stories we've heard others tell of hovering over their beds in hospitals and then coming back into their bodies? Sherry, together we can believe. God will answer that. It's His Word. Make it happen, honey, now! Tell Him it's not your time. Sherry, I love you, you know that. I didn't mean for this to happen. Sherry, please!!! I love you, you know I do. Sherry, please, don't leave me, don't do this to me, to us!!"

I did not want to stop touching her, or I knew they would make me leave. "Honey, I love you. They've taken all your clothes off, except for your panties. That would embarrass you, someone seeing your breasts. The damn ambulance crew—they didn't need to cut your blouse open. At least your panties are on and they aren't the Harley set I gave you as a joke. That really would be an embarrassment for you."

Holding her feet with her partially webbed toes, I said, "You don't belong under this sheet. At least you won't have cold feet anymore; you always complained about being cold. If I turn around they'll make me leave. I feel them looking at me. Can you come back if I leave or does that make it final? An elder and a deacon just got here to be with me and you're still dead. How can that be? I don't want to leave you, but it's time, I guess."

As we pulled into my driveway, I hoped the lights from the police car would not wake the girls. They were going to need all the sleep they could get. They were going to need all the strength they had and more. "God, please stop this," I begged, but it didn't stop and I couldn't figure out why.

I could not figure any of this out because I was in the first phase of the grief cycle, which is the sudden shock you feel when confronted with the situation. Any major trauma can push you into this phase. When the shock comes, you will be screaming "No!" to the situation. _This cannot be_ will shout in your head. You will demand that everything stop and return to what it was, normal. You will actually expect this to happen.

When someone tries to soothe and calm you down, you will not listen because you will not want to hear it. The words will not register with you. You will be too focused on trying to get your life back to what it was just a few minutes, hours, or days before. Reality cannot get through to you at this point. You are in shock.

Having to notify Sherry's family was so hard. I couldn't let them find it out on the morning news, secondhand. _How do I tell her father, who trusts God and loves his daughter? How do I find the right words?_ These questions kept going round and round in my mind.

At 7 a.m. people started arriving at the house. I knew the cars were going to wake the girls, and sure enough, there both of them stood, looking at me, full of questions. They knew something was wrong. Rebekah asked, "Who died? Was it Grandpa? Uncle Bill? Who?"

"Girls, we need to go upstairs to talk," I said as I led them from the room. Oh, the innocence in their faces and the fear in their eyes. Again I wondered, _How do I find the_ *right words?* Then I realized, there were no right words. What had happened was not right in any way, yet it was reality.

As I sat on Elisabeth's bed, I knew sitting there would never be the same again. They did not want to hear what I had to tell them. "Girls, what I'm going to tell you is going to hurt so you need to be prepared. Your mother and I were coming home on the motorcycle last night and we had a wreck." Immediately Rebekah interrupted me and tremblingly asked, "Where's Mom?" I looked directly at them and said, "Girls, there were four of us and now there are only three."

God help me, I could not bear the piercing scream that came from Libby. How could that horrible noise be coming from that sweet face? I can still hear Rebekah shouting, "No!" There was no way to stop them from hurting, and wasn't that my job as their father, to make sure nothing ever hurt them like this? Now not only were they being hurt, but I was the one inflicting the hurt by telling them this horrible news.

Their screams seemed to go on forever. Their comments and questions were coming too fast for me to answer: "I didn't get to tell Mommy good-bye last night. Did she say anything? Where is she? Can we see her?" I just sat there. "I'm sorry, so sorry," was all I could say, and I kept repeating it over and over. They wouldn't let me hold them, so I sat there, helpless to do anything to assuage their grief. God, how I wished I'd died.

We had a private viewing, just my daughters and me. How ominous and sinister, yet antiseptically clean, the viewing room was. We stood there with the doors closed, just the three of us. I had an arm around each of them. We didn't know what to do, how to act, or what to say. The girls approached the casket and looked at their mother.

No one knows what to say at these times. The shock has enveloped you and your mind is attempting to do the impossible—compute the information you have been confronted with. You are just not wired to do this. It's impossible, it's inconceivable, it's just not happening. "No" is the response when you are in shock. No to accepting what has happened, no to discussing it as if it is a reality and no to trying to make any sense out of something that you are so sure is not going to last.

A thousand thoughts dart through your mind, but it's unable to function properly. You can see, hear, listen, and even make decisions, but not with any clarity. Everything seems detached and indifferent. It's like groping for stability that is just out of your reach. You know the stability should be there, but it's not, and you have this nagging feeling that it never will be again. You're afraid, so you just keep insisting that things _will_ go back to normal.

Libby touched Sherry and wanted to know why she felt " hard." She then pulled out a piece of cloth she had sewn. It read, "Thank you for being a good mother," and she laid it across Sherry's arms. Again, that feeling of helplessness washed over me. I could do nothing to stop what was happening.

How do you say a final good-bye to your wife, friend, lover, and soul mate, the person you love and have become one with? Walking out of the funeral home felt like such a violation and betrayal of my allegiance to Sherry and my faith. That night I had an "encounter" with her voice. She urged me to "be strong and courageous." I woke with a start and jumped out of bed to embrace her. I hugged the wall where her voice seemed to be coming from, but could not bring her back. God, it hurt so much.

It was such a vivid experience that I tried to share it with Libby, not even thinking of the effect it might have on her. She immediately started crying, and wanted to know why Sherry hadn't come and talked to her, since she hadn't been able to tell her mother good-bye. I could see how hurt she was, having heard this, and I felt so bad that I had just inflicted more pain. I didn't bring the occurrence up again.

I am well aware of the theological teachings on whether the dead can or cannot communicate with the living. But I am also personally familiar with the hell and torment that night brings to those in the throes of grief—the overwhelming desire to talk to and be with the loved one. Whether it is the recounting of voices heard or a presence sensed, these occurrences seem to happen to countless intelligent, stable people. We would neither deny nor encourage this, but would let the bereaved hold to their perception of the experience. The encounter so often gives comfort, which is so badly needed at this time.

I didn't know you could go to a funeral parlor and shop for caskets. There seemed to be row upon row of them. It was like shopping in Wal-Mart, but for dead people. When I entered the room and saw all that was available, I realized I was going to put my wife into the ground. This was going to be final. It was becoming real. My knees were undependable, and I looked for a place to sit down. The funeral director and my father were saying something to me, but all I knew was I wanted out of there!

I chose one of the cheapest caskets and a flat stone in the colors Sherry would have liked. Later I wished I had chosen an upright stone. She deserved better than a flat stone. I had part of her favorite Scripture verse inscribed on it, "A Tree of Righteousness"—and then later wished I had put her Christian bookstore name, "Flower of the Field," on it instead. There are so many things you do at the time of the death that later you wish you had done differently, but the fact is that you did the best you could at the time. Remember that—you did the best you could.

Walking into the funeral home and viewing Sherry's body was surreal to say the least, but it was also a step toward handling the grief. It is an oxymoron, but you have to hurt before you can begin to heal. I needed to realize that death had taken place, and that realization came with viewing the body. The close, loving good-byes that followed also helped to make it real.

It was the breaking of earthly ties that had to take place. It was also a final picture that will be burned into my mind forever. I'm glad we took the opportunity and the time for personal, departing words. Doing this was my first step toward healing. Whatever ritual you choose to engage in to say a final farewell to your loved one will also be your first, needed step toward healing. Of course, at this time, you don't want to hear the word "healing" or anything about recovering, you want your loved one back! The thought of healing seems obscene at this time.

I gave Sherry's funeral. It was the way she had said she would want it. The church was full of believers and nonbelievers. "Rejoicing and salvation" were the themes for the day, just like we were taught and had believed. The trouble was, it was hollow. A funeral should memorialize the deceased and comfort the family. Instead, hope is slipping away and the loved one is departing. Those closest to the deceased are incapacitated by their anguish, and they often fail to hear anything that's being said.

My heart ached while my mind wandered. I had held her feet while in the emergency room; that was the last time I had touched her. She had trusted me. She hated being on that bike, but got on it anyway. She was determined to be part of everything I was involved in. It had happened on a Tuesday night. She should have been home preparing the Christian school curriculum for the following day. She wasn't at school that next day. She had never before missed school, and now she would never be there again. It just wasn't right, not any part of it, yet it was reality now.

It was just three days after the death and I didn't want to see anyone, yet there I was at the funeral and the church was full. Pastors always want full churches, but now it meant nothing to me. It seemed crazy to be singing praise songs at a funeral, but that's what she said she wanted when we would talk about what our funerals would be like "someday." Now all those glorious proclamations seemed so empty, so mocking.

There were plenty of bikers with their women there too. *Maybe,* I thought, *they will get saved and make it worthwhile.* But then I thought, *Nothing was worth this. I wouldn't trade her for the salvation of all the bikers in the world.* At this time, the "call" to save people certainly was not worth the personal loss of my wife.

I could not focus on anything. Years later someone asked me if, looking back at that time, I had not felt that I still had spiritual responsibilities, since I was continuing to pastor the church. The answer is that during grief all your responsibilities are starkly evident to you, but fulfilling most of them is a challenge because of your inability to focus. I thought, up to the time of Sherry's death, that the church was my life, but I now knew my wife had been my life. I continued to fulfill my ministerial responsibilities, but my heart was no longer in it. I felt as though my heart had stopped beating.

3

Kathy's Story

It was late in the afternoon when the phone rang. "Mrs. Serefine, this is the YMCA calling. Don't panic, but your husband is having trouble breathing." I asked if he had lost consciousness (*How did I know to ask that?* I wondered later), and they replied that he had. They asked me to go immediately to the hospital.

The ride there was grueling, it seemed to take forever! I was driving behind an old man who would go no faster than 30 mph—on a country road!—and there was no opportunity to pass him. When I finally got into the city, and was a block from the hospital, I entered a school zone and was then stuck behind some law-abiding citizen who went the speed limit of just 15 mph. My emotions and thoughts ran back and forth between *Calm down, it's probably nothing* to the worst possible scenarios.

Upon arriving at the emergency room, I was met by a nurse who had grown up with Jerry. I was to discover later that not only was she an incredible nurse but a pretty good actress too. Mary Jo told me that she had seen them bring

Jerry in, but had no idea how he was. She directed me to a private waiting room. This was a room, I found out later, where they always put people who are going to be told of the death of a loved one.

She told me that it would probably be a long wait until we heard something, and she asked if there were any friends I could call who might come and sit with me until then. Unsuspectingly, I gave her the names of two close friends and she called them. She waited with me until they arrived, and then casually said she would go see if she could get some information on Jerry's condition. I found out later that this is when she informed the doctor that I could now be told the truth about my husband—that he was dead.

The doctor entered the room, followed by Mary Jo. The first thing I noticed was that Mary Jo was crying. At the same time, the doctor started saying these horrible words: "Mrs. Serefine, I did all I could for your husband; I'm sorry, but he's dead." I immediately jumped up and screamed at this virtual stranger, "You're lying to me, you are *lying to me!!!* Stop it!! Jerry would not do that to me. He's only 40. He can't be dead, so just stop it!!!"

I then told them—no, dared them—to take me to him. I had to see him with my own eyes or I wouldn't believe it was true. I just knew Jerry would never die and leave me alone. Although they tried to discourage me, I was adamant. The moment I saw him, however, all doubts were gone. He was most certainly dead. My husband was dead.

Jerry was not a conceited man, but he would never have let anyone see him looking so ghastly. I just stared at him in shock, and suddenly *my* entire future passed before my eyes. I saw our children, Rachel, 14, and Bud, 10, graduating from school, getting married, accomplishing things, enjoying life, and he would miss all of it! The only thing I could say, over and over, was, "I'm so sorry, baby." There was so much meaning in those words. I was so sorry for all that was to come that Jerry and I would never get to share together.

As I stood there stroking his forehead, I finally realized I had to go. My mind was numb. It didn't feel right to be leaving, yet there was no reason to stay. I had never felt so utterly alone before. I felt as though my whole body had suffered an electrical shock. It was actually buzzing. It was like a "Twilight Zone" episode where everything looks normal, but slightly crooked and out of focus.

It was not at all like when my dad had died. At that time, I had Jerry to turn to for comfort. He took care of everything. Now I had to be the one to "take care of everything," whatever that meant. My first thought was, *How do I tell the kids?* They knew I had been called to the hospital, but as I left the house I had tried to minimize what was happening. So now how was I supposed to do it? My friend Joe said to make it short and to the point: "At 6:10 tonight your dad died of a heart attack while exercising at the YMCA."

The screaming was more than I could bear. They would not let me touch them. I had no comfort to give them anyway, so I just sat there feeling empty. Their protection from the world was gone. I was now that protection, but at the same time, I was giving them the worst news they had ever heard. What a laugh—I was all they had! That realization scared me so much. I felt like a house with the roof blown off, totally exposed.

We had a private viewing before the wake, and it was pitiful to see the kids physically yearn for their father. I just stood watching them, so helpless to give them what they could never have again—their dad. The word *inadequate* took on new meaning for me. I knew the best I could give them at that point was the experience of a wake so they could meet all the people who had loved and respected their father. They heard some wonderful things about their dad at the wake from a variety of people whom they otherwise would never have met.

After the funeral, after the spreading of his ashes, and after a couple of weeks, life began returning to normal for everyone but us. For us, normal was a continuing nightmare. I was a woman whose life had centered around her husband, and I was a teacher now on summer vacation. For me, it was beyond being a nightmare. There are no words to fully describe it.

The question that continually haunted me was, *Why are we allowed to love so much only to lose so badly?* I never got an answer. I realized that Jerry never knew how much I loved him, because I didn't know it myself until after he died. I didn't know it was possible to love someone that deeply. There was no comfort anywhere. The only one who could truly comfort me was gone and could not come back. That was becoming increasingly clear, and it was just unacceptable. There was nothing I could do to fix it. Frustration was constant within me.

Just a few weeks after Jerry's death, I began to feel tremendous guilt about how needy I had become. I just seemed to suck the life out of people and had nothing to give in return. To complicate matters, my mother passed away 11 months later.

Mom had been sick with emphysema for six years, but she had been a rock of comfort for me after Jerry died. Having been widowed herself, she brought special understanding to my situation. We became closer than ever during her last year of life. I sought her advice about everything. Consequently, when she died, a tremendous source of strength and understanding was torn away from me at my most desperate time. Interestingly, however, I did not go into deep grief at my mother's passing. I guess it was because I was so very relieved that she was finally out of distress. For six years I had watched her gasp for every breath. I had also watched her slowly deteriorate until finally she was entirely bedridden.

I remember, at her funeral, giving thanks to God that He had finally released her from this life. Imagine my surprise, then, when six months later I was in a store, saw some cards she would have liked, decided to buy them for her, and suddenly was hit with the full realization that my mother was dead. Suddenly it didn't matter that she had been old and sick and was now in a better place. She was my mother and I wanted her with me! I was consumed with grief. This overwhelming grief caught me totally off guard. I thought I had dealt with it at the time of her funeral. The truth was that the grief had only been delayed. I now had not only my husband's death to grieve, but also my mother's.

We're often asked the question: is grieving for an unexpected death the same as grieving for an anticipated death? Both are filled with pain. With anticipated loss, you often get to say good-bye and set your affairs in order. At first this would appear to be a more desirable way to die. However, after the fact, the grief is still the same for the survivors. It is devastating.

With the additional grief of my mother's death, I became even more aware of how needy I was. At the same time, I felt helpless to do anything about it. I felt completely misunderstood and alone. One of the reasons Jerry's death was so impossible for me to bear was that at age 40, none of my friends had been through the death of a spouse, so I had no contemporary to commiserate with.

So, on my own, I tried to figure it all out. On my own, I tried to give my children guidance. On my own I tried to get our lives on track. On my own did not go well for me at all. I didn't know how to be on my own. I had gone from being Daddy's little girl to Jerry's little wife—and I had been so good at it too! I was a 1950s kind of obedient wife. I always deferred to Jerry, so I had a very hard time accepting my new role of being in charge, being the decision-maker. I had to learn how to be independent, and more importantly, how to be comfortable with it.

I remember my first shaky steps toward attaining this independence. I had to pay the bills! I had to write checks! I had to balance Jerry's checkbook, which had now become my checkbook! Before his death, I had written only one check a week, and that was for groceries. This was *quite* an experience for me.

When I think back on that time, I remember what a pitiful person I was—sitting at the table, writing checks and crying, always crying! I cried not only because I missed Jerry so much, but also because of all the unknowns that the future held. I was really scared of all the responsibility facing me. I remember sitting there thinking, *If writing checks scares me, then how am I ever going to handle all those other "grown-up things" that are expected of me?* I had never had a problem with Jerry being the decision-maker, the one in charge. I didn't want that responsibility, yet suddenly I had it, and it completely overwhelmed me.

My sense of trust toward life had been destroyed when Jerry died. This opened the door for fear to take over, and it did! The death made me realize that I had no real control over anything in my life. I now knew that circumstances could change things permanently in just an instant, and sometimes there was just no solution when that happened. This lack of trust colored my entire belief system. I was afraid to trust anyone but myself, and I didn't have much confidence in me.

4

The Agony of Grief

The previous two chapters dealt with the trauma both of us experienced as we worked our way through the shock phase of the grief cycle. On the heels of this, we both, in our own way, entered the agony phase of grief. Webster's defines agony as the intense pain of both the mind and the body. You feel as though all your nerve endings are exposed, and you are bathed in pain. It just disables you. It's so overpowering that nothing previously experienced can possibly prepare you for the intensity of it. It seems never-ending, and while you're in the worst of it, you may feel that if it continues just one more minute, you're going to crawl right out of your skin. Then, unbelievably, it does continue—but you stay inside your skin anyway.

For many people, the agony phase takes the form of restlessness. When this happens you feel that you have to keep moving, yet you're not comfortable anywhere you go. Your mind is on overload and seems about ready to short-circuit. You have been robbed of your significance.

When you feel significant, you feel special—you feel that you count for something. The person who died helped give you that significance, helped to make you feel important. Also, you gave significance to that person. You cared for, worried about, and loved him or her. Now, all that is gone, and you feel so alone and insignificant. You still have all this love and caring in you, but you don't have that person to give it to.

During this phase, thoughts of your loved one will become an obsession. You'll agonize endlessly over small details of your life together, and reminders of the past will make you feel as though you're there all over again. You'll want to straighten out your thinking, but find it impossible to do much of the time. You may want to talk about the loved one incessantly—when you talk at all. This helps to re-establish your significance, as well as the significance of the one you've lost.

We have found in working with grieving people that when we ask the question, "How did you meet your spouse?" their faces will light up. They will smile and sometimes even laugh, as they will go into great detail about the event. During their brief recounting of their courtship and subsequent marriage, they will feel alive, significant, once again. Their loved one seems to be with them.

It's also during the agony phase of grief that the "what ifs" come: What if we hadn't gone there? What if we had spent more time together? etc., etc. The "what ifs" can become a springboard to blame. You may blame yourself, and/or you may blame the very person you loved the most, the one who died. You may blame others who give advice or who are trying to help. If you do blame them, it is because you think they don't know the situation or understand what you're really feeling. Your entire life seems shrouded in misery and sorrow. It's kind of like living in a portable coffin. You're not dead, but you don't really feel alive either.

The agony phase seems to afflict people most at night or during the quiet times. Those around you care, but the agony of your grief makes it very hard to receive their comfort. The only one who can truly comfort you is irrevocably gone, and there is nothing you can do to fix that. You want things to return to normal, but they just don't. You realize that the situation has no solution, and you find this unacceptable.

During this phase, you also realize the secondary losses you have suffered because of the death. Secondary losses could include things such as social standing, income, and friends. For example, while I (Kathy) was married to Jerry, he had a high-profile job with the local school district. He knew everyone in town. A few months after his death, I saw some of the movers and shakers of the town who had known Jerry, and they passed me right by without so much as a glance.

The truth was, they had no idea who I was. They had seen me with Jerry and always treated me graciously, but it was really him they knew, not me. Without him, I now felt invisible. So in addition to mourning Jerry, I now had to mourn my loss of social status in the community. This is a typical situation for a lot of women.

A woman we counseled was in deep despair. She was a stay-at-home mom and had never worked. Her children were all grown, and her husband had died suddenly. She discovered after he died that he did not have sufficient insurance, so she had to sell her home and get a job for the first time in her 56 years. In addition to mourning her husband, she had to mourn the loss of her home as well as her lifestyle.

The agony phase of grief robs you of your self-confidence and damages your sense of trust. You have received such a blow from life, how can you dare trust again? This hurt travels from your head to your heart and back again. In every other difficult situation, we work through it and put it behind us. This is impossible to do with the death of a loved one. There is no truer saying than "Where there's life, there's hope." That's what makes accepting the death so hard. The person is no longer alive, so there seems to be no hope anywhere, only agony. You'll never get another chance to be with that person, and that is the hardest part to accept.

One of the worst times in the agony phase came for me (Kathy) two months and four days after Jerry's death. I had gone to his office that morning to bring his things home. They all fit into one small box. I brought the box into the house and put it in the dining room. Throughout the day, as I would walk through the dining room, I would glance over at the box and think to myself, *Ten years in that job and it all fits in one box, huh, Jer? Ten long years and that's all you get—one box!* As I looked at the box, I found myself growing increasingly sadder, and slowly my sadness turned to anger. Finally, by that night, ugly bitterness had set in.

I started thinking about how futile life was. I could think of no reason to go on any longer. I saw no hope in any area of my life. As far as I was concerned, life was something I was now being forced to endure, and I was tired of it. One of my biggest problems since Jerry's death had been that I couldn't sleep for more than an hour or two at night. The doctors had given me two prescriptions for sleeping pills right after the death. So I got those pills out of my purse, and when my friend Barb walked into my living room, I was sitting on the couch, staring at them. I was thinking, _Why not end it all? Someone will take the kids, there's always someone to take care of things. I can just take these pills, go to sleep, and be with Jerry again._ It seemed like the perfect solution. Barb took one look at me and knew what I was thinking.

She told me I had to call Mark. He had sent me a card after Jerry died and offered to talk with me, since he had been through the same situation. Barb had been very good to me, seeing me daily and always being ready to listen, but she just did not know what to say anymore. She was sure Mark could help. Since she was so insistent, I decided to call him. I figured I could always kill myself the next day.

Mark and I had never met before that night. We lived in the same neighborhood, and had in fact moved into town on the exact same day seven years previous. He had known Jerry, but we had never met. After we introduced ourselves, I looked at him and said, "I want to die." His simple reply was, "I know you do; let's talk."

For the next three hours, that's exactly what we did. We sat and talked, with me doing most of the talking. Since he was a total stranger, I figured I would just let it all out. My thinking was, _Hey, I've never seen this guy before, I'll probably never see him again._ So I told him everything about my relationship with Jerry. I told him that basically Jerry and I had one big marital problem—he had died. Other than that, we had enjoyed a good marriage.

Talking truthfully with Mark helped as I struggled with my grief. I was able to examine the pain with someone who had been where I now found myself. For example, with Mark's help I realized it was little things that would catch my attention for a brief moment and then propel me into the agony phase. It would be things like the way one person in a couple would reach out to touch the other, or seeing the way someone tossed his head to the side or walked just the way Jerry did. These instant reminders seemed to be continually appearing and reminding me of my lost life. The box I had brought home that day from his office had served as the catalyst on this particular night.

I (Mark) understood Kathy's feelings, not only because I had experienced them myself, but also because I had observed them in other people. For example, while I was speaking to a church group in Dallas, a lady who had lost her husband in a car accident just three months before was introduced to me. Her relatives didn't know what to do with her. They knew of my situation and wanted me to counsel her. I told her that she was still in shock and the worst was yet to come. Her relatives looked at me as though I were saying something dirty and disgusting.

She asked me if it was going to get better. I told her that it was going to get worse before it got better, that it was going to be the closest thing to hell she would ever experience. Her relatives did *not* want to hear this. I think at this point they would have liked to take me out to the parking lot and stone me. Thank God it was asphalt! Their idea was for me to perform an instant miracle to heal her. They were totally upset with me.

A year later this lady called me and said that when she went through the hell I had warned her about, she knew she wasn't losing her mind. Because of my total honesty, she felt I had helped save her sanity. She knew from what I had said that she wasn't the only one in the world to experience this kind of pain.

When we facilitate grief groups for Hospice, one of our goals is to get people to explore their grief from many different perspectives. One way to accomplish this is to ask them to tell us what a picture of their grief would look like. We get a variety of responses. They range from grief looking like a deep, bottomless pit to it being made up of vivid colors colliding together in the shape of a bolt of lightning. One man said, "How do you paint a picture of something so ugly?" I (Kathy) see it as a person sitting alone in a rowboat, drifting farther and farther from shore. People on the shore, can't seem to reach the person in the boat. The person just sits motionless, staring into space.

When you're in the agony phase of grief, you may think you're really losing your mind. It's not a matter of saying, "Keep a stiff upper lip and stop feeling this way." It's more a matter of literally feeling that you cannot go on. Observers may not realize it but for the first year or so after the death, you really are trying to do the best you can but you're very much aware that it's not as good as it was before the death. However, it's the best you have to offer.

I (Kathy) had an experience one year after Jerry died that illustrates this point perfectly. I had returned to my teaching job just three months after Jerry's death. Understandably, the school year had been rough for me. A lot had obviously changed in my life. For one thing, I married Mark eight months after the death. With my remarriage came harsh criticism from people who were sure they would have done things differently had they been me.

These people had no idea of the reality of my life, nor did they really care, except to gossip and judge. As my mother told me when we discussed my remarrying, "If you are going to do something out of the norm, then be prepared for the firestorm of gossip that will accompany it." My mother was right!

My mother died three months after my remarriage, and eleven months after Jerry. To lose a mother and a husband all in one year was more than anyone should have to bear. This multiple loss magnified and complicated everything.

A month after my mother's death I was called into my principal's office. He told me that they were transferring me to another building because I hadn't been a very good team player that year. He voiced his confusion over why I had even come back to work, as well as to why I had lost so much weight. The truth was that I had begun to diet before Jerry died. I needed to lose weight. After his death, I couldn't seem to find my appetite, so I continued to lose additional pounds. I had finally reached my goal weight and was comfortable with it. I thought I looked fine.

He also told me that my co-workers were concerned and uncomfortable around me because I didn't go in the teacher's room as often as I used to, and I stayed in my room alone too much. He told me my colleagues had discussed this, and it had been decided that a transfer was the best thing for me. These meetings had taken place without my knowledge, and I had no chance to provide input.

I had gotten paranoid during that first year anyway. I thought everyone was watching me and talking about me. In my saner moments, I would tell myself to stop it, that I was not that important for people to be watching me. Now my principal had just reinforced my paranoid thoughts. As they say, just because you're paranoid doesn't mean people *aren't* watching you. He then said there were other concerns, but he didn't want to "get specific." So not only was he kicking me out of the building, but he wasn't going to give me the "other" reasons why. This, obviously, wasn't the best way for him to handle this situation, but I must say that his timing was exquisite. He had chosen the day before the one-year anniversary of Jerry's death to drop this bombshell on me. All I could do was sit there and cry. The fact was, I had done the best I could that year.

The agony phase of the grief cycle may be the hardest phase for some people to go through. You are in such mental pain that problems can become magnified. I often thought I literally would not survive when I found myself in this phase.

5

The Negative Response

When children argue, one of them will sometimes say to the other, "I wish you'd die." Upon hearing this, an adult will tell the child that this is a terrible thing to say. In reality, that really isn't the most terrible thing you can wish on someone. The cruelest thing is instead to wish they'd lose the one they love most. That is the worst pain there is. It is a pain that can bring about all sorts of negative responses.

A negative response isn't always an angry one. Many times it's experienced as depression or loneliness. It's healthy to identify the emotion for what it is and to be honest about it. Negative responses sometimes manifest themselves in the following areas:

1. Radical religious involvement. This generally causes you to seek "deep" spiritual answers. The "hidden" meaning of life and death are dwelled upon. Not only is there a desire to be close to God, but there is the consuming desire to see God in

everything. Others may turn away from you and consider you a "religious fanatic."

2. Promiscuity. Different thoughts attempt to justify this, such as, *I played by the rules the first time and lost, so why not?* or, *I've lost my partner, so I'll have sex with whomever I choose.* There is such a need for a personal touch, a caring relationship, emotional fulfillment, the understanding that can only be met by closeness.

3. Turning to drugs (legal or illegal) and/or alcohol. There is a need to numb the emotional feelings and to distance yourself from their destruction. Logic has no place here. There is just the prevailing longing to stop the thoughts and feelings that are crushing your soul mentally and emotionally.

4. Suicidal thoughts and personality changes. A quiet person may become talkative, or an outgoing person may become introspective. Personal habits might change. You may find yourself sleeping all the time, or rarely sleeping at all.

There is nothing shameful about the negative response. You don't need to hide it or see it as a sign of weakness. As a matter of fact, using it properly can help you regain your mental health. Anger can benefit you: it eliminates apathy and releases bottled-up negative energy. It can give you new insights, and might spur you into taking steps to make some necessary changes in your life. These changes might include opening up communication with people who are a challenge to relate with or removing things from your life that you can't deal with at this point.

For example, I (Kathy) was painting trim on a rental house Jerry and I had bought shortly before his death. I was apprehensive about buying the house to begin with but after much discussion, Jerry convinced me that we should. He told me I wouldn't have to do a thing with it, that he would always take care of it. Within two months of his death, our tenants moved out. So there I was, trying to get it ready to rent again, and I was _mad!_

I was so angry that at one parent I picked up an almost full bucket of paint and flung it at the house as I screamed in frustration. All it did was embarrass me. I told Mark about it, and he helped me understand that it was all right to be angry, that I needed to express it.

He pointed out that if I repressed the anger, it would most likely turn into depression which is really just anger without energy. When I finally accepted that anger is a normal part of the grieving process, I knew I could stop feeling guilty about it and, more importantly, stop denying how angry I was at Jerry, and everything else.

As I thought about Mark's observation about anger turning into depression if not expressed, I realized that although I had never been prone to depression, it now seemed to be a constant in my life. I had to admit to myself that I had been repressing a lot of anger, and it was growing. Before Jerry's death I was always such an optimist, but the hard realities confronting me now made optimism a thing of the past.

For example, I didn't know until the death that you could physically feel pain from a broken heart. I didn't know I could cry so many tears and still have more to shed. Depression became like an ugly friend, and I had to get rid of it.

If you get depressed, you feel so isolated, and you think no one understands. In a sense this is true; no one does. How can they? Only you know your thoughts and feelings. Everything seems backward or upside down. Things often don't appear real or lasting, because you now know that they can change in an instant, and there is nothing you can do about it.

Things I (Kathy) assumed would bother me after Jerry died didn't—like still working out at the YMCA where he had died. However, going to the grocery store was more than I could bear. Everything I bought was connected to him, and brought back unbearable memories.

One Saturday night I (Mark) got drunk. I didn't normally drink, but I just didn't care anymore. I wanted to stop hurting and thinking so much. The following morning at church, a faithful friend took me aside. He told me that if I was going to get drunk, I really shouldn't do it the night before church, because I reeked! I had made sure to drink only at home after my daughters were in bed, so no one would know. I thought I wouldn't tarnish my image this way. Suddenly my secret was exposed.

I (Mark) also had an overwhelming desire to commit suicide. One morning at 5:30 a.m., I was sitting on my porch steps, in my underwear, my heart broken, my head wanting the hurt to stop, and knowing the .38-caliber Smith & Wesson pistol I was holding would put an end to it all. I didn't fear eternity or the afterlife, or even contemplate what God thought about it. I didn't care in the least. My only question was, who would care for my daughters? I could not bear thinking of them hurting any more than they already were.

I concluded that for as little good as I felt I could do them, I still needed to be around to try to help them. My next illogical thought was, *Why not just kill them too?* But I knew I couldn't hurt them, so I just sat there, dying inside.

I (Kathy) used to go into my closet and bury my face in Jerry's clothes, just to smell him. One day I did this and his smell had faded. The brief comfort I had gotten from this was now gone, so that was the day I got rid of all his clothes. It seemed there was betrayal all around me—his death, perceived abandonment by friends, and now old comforts fading away.

I (Mark) began suspecting that I hated God, but because of all my taught theology as a minister I kept repressing these thoughts. I would be counseled regularly not to blame God, and I would automatically reply, "I'm not blaming God, leave me alone." Then one Saturday, when the church was empty except for me, I stood up and shouted, "God, I hate you! I hate you, I hate you!!" And I meant it with all my being. Death had split my family, and this mighty God I served so faithfully had done nothing to prevent it. When I told this to people, they were shocked and couldn't believe I would do that in church, but why not? God already knew what I was thinking anyway. God is always ready for a heart-to-heart.

It was two months into the negative response phase of my grief, and I (Mark) was becoming angrier all the time. I was also bitter and spiteful. I hated anybody who had ever dared to speak against Sherry! This ate at me. I either had to conquer it or resign from the ministry. I was forced to humble myself and address the issue with my congregation. I told them that I needed their help, and then I shared the depth of my pain as best I could. They were very surprised because I had been so skillful at disguising my pain. They had never suspected that it went that deep or hurt that much, or that I was that ugly. They completely supported me.

My (Kathy) most devastating encounter with the negative response occurred two years after Jerry's death. Because of what I perceived as our special relationship, I just knew that he would come back to see me, if only for a few moments. Maybe no one else's spouse had ever came back, but I *knew* it would be different for us. I was confident it would happen when he knew I could handle seeing him again. On the second anniversary of his death, I told myself he would definitely come then. It seemed logical because I had now grieved to the point where hysteria was no longer an issue. I knew I could see him briefly and then let him go.

I went to the place where I had spread his ashes, a bluff overlooking Keuka Lake, and waited. I was absolutely heartbroken when he didn't appear. Fortunately no one was around, because I became hysterical. Since I was up there all alone, I really let it all out—I screamed, kicked my car, and literally jumped up and down. Did it make me feel better? Not at all, it only left me feeling very depressed.

It is important to recognize any anger or depression issues you might find yourself struggling with. We cannot stress enough that you need to take steps to rid yourself of them. Anger issues can create a no-win situation for people who have to interact with you. For example, a woman goes to her hairdresser soon after she has suffered a loss and is asked how she is. She replies, "How do you *think* I am?" The next time she goes to get her hair cut, the hairdresser doesn't dare ask how she is. The woman gets angry and thinks to herself, *I can't believe she doesn't care enough to even wonder how I am.*

It is not a sign of weakness to admit that you're angry or depressed. We can get so righteous when we're dressed properly and it's daylight and the secrets of our hearts are hidden, but that doesn't negate the fact that we're hurting on the inside. Acknowledging these negative responses is the first step toward finding a solution for them and letting the hurt begin to heal. Remember, anger is healthy and natural. Only by getting in touch with it can you take control of it—instead of it controlling you.

6

The Positive Response
and Boundaries

Healthy mental, emotional, and physical boundaries are a key to having positive responses in your life. The person who sets boundaries has a feeling of well-being and self-confidence. He has a clear concept of what he will and won't accept in his life. He is in control of his life, yet not controlling of others.

A good way to understand boundaries is to visualize your life as a cell. The boundaries you put in place are like the membrane that surrounds and protects the cell. This membrane, or boundary, is flexible, and allows only healthy things in while keeping toxic things out. With healthy boundaries, you can continue to grow while remaining flexible. You'll be better able to discern which situations and people are healthy, and which are toxic.

By establishing clear boundaries and living by them, you will grow in confidence. The strength you'll feel will be exhilarating. Once firmly in place, your boundaries will liberate and empower you. However, this empowerment has dual consequences. While it does feel liberating, it's also a little threatening. You're enabling yourself to be in control and independent. You're stepping out of your old comfort zone into a new one that you have created. You're flying solo, perhaps for the first time in your life. To be effective, your boundaries should be like fences with gates. They must be flexible and allow for change. For example, don't make "rules." Instead, devise "principles" that cover a wider range of situations. Rules don't apply in every circumstance, but principles do.

The added bonus of healthy boundaries is that they will gradually free you from the despondency of the past. You will develop a new awareness that you are no longer the victim, but are becoming an overcomer. Healthy boundaries free you from black-and-white statements filled with absolutes like "always," "everybody," "must," or "should." Remember, stay flexible and stay in charge. Choose to exercise your boundaries on a daily basis. Research shows that it takes about three to four weeks for something to become a habit, so that's approximately how long it will take for you to feel comfortable with your new boundaries. They will eventually become part of who you are, and then you will feel comfortably in control of your life.

Healthy boundaries help you determine who gets close to you and who doesn't. This may sound odd, but you need to surround yourself with "safe" people. These are the people who listen to you *and* accept your opinions and feelings. They're honest and supportive. You have inner peace after spending time with them and sharing your thoughts and feelings.

People who make you feel just the opposite are toxic people and codependents. A codependent is a person who needs to control and fix people or situations. He has low self-esteem and, quite often, immaturity issues. He believes that his happiness hinges on others, and he feels responsible for them. The codependent worries about things he can't change, but tries his best to change them anyway, usually with disappointing results. His life is ruled by extremes. He subconsciously is looking for what's missing or lacking in his own life.

When you're feeling defeated, a codependent may enter your life and start trying to control it. At first his advice will be very welcome because you're so devastated and need someone to lean on. It will be a relief that someone cares so much. He'll start "fixing" your life and you'll respond positively to it. Things will be running smoothly, and you'll be grateful for all he is doing.

The codependent may begin to mesh his life with yours. Thus, you become codependent with him or literally dependent on him. This works fine for a while. The trouble starts when you begin to regain your strength and make decisions that the codependent disagrees with. He will become judgmental and critical.

One person who assumed this position in my (Kathy's) life was such a comfort to me at first. She dealt with all the minor details of my life so I wouldn't have to be burdened with them. She handled difficult people for me on the phone, and she spent lots of time with my kids so I could take time for myself. I appreciated her efforts so much. However, one evening when my son asked if I was all right, she yelled at him. She told him to stop badgering me. I could not believe she would do that and told her to stop it. My son was only expressing his concern and anxiety. She threw her hands up in disgust and in an exasperated tone of voice told me that she was only trying to "put this family back together again."

I tried to tell her that this wasn't her job, but she got very angry. I was stunned at her reaction. She had been so understanding at first, but suddenly she seemed to be using all I had confided in her as proof that she knew what was best for me. It scared me because I had not seen it coming at all.

My sisters were the exact opposite. They were "safe" people. We were in almost daily contact by phone. I would bounce different ideas off them and they would simply encourage me to do what I thought was best. Sure, they would give me an opinion *if* I asked for it, but I always knew it was only that, an opinion, not an order to do what they said. They never presumed to know what was best for me.

As soon as you can, identify any codependency problems in your life. Beware of the advice-giver. He could be a codependent who lacks fulfillment in his own life and is searching for self-importance, self-acceptance, and control in yours. Control is central to a codependent's life. A healthy person who offers help will applaud your progress, encourage you to keep on striving, and support you in your boundary-setting.

Setting up healthy boundaries is crucial for recovering and establishing direction in your life. The first step is to start thinking healthy thoughts, which is easier said than done. You must make a conscious effort to replace defeating thoughts with positive ones. When you find you are doing this more than just occasionally, you have definitely reached the positive response phase in the grief cycle.

You'll also know that you've reached the positive response phase when you can finally recognize the reality and finality of the death. At this point, you will have reestablished stable eating and sleeping patterns. You will be enjoying new experiences, and not feeling guilty because you're continuing to live. You will actually organize and plan for the future, and you'll be able to acknowledge new parts of yourself that developed during your grief journey. One of the best signs that you have reached this phase is when you rediscover your sense of humor. It isn't being disloyal to your loved one to find that you're able to laugh once again.

Suffering is an easy trait to keep, but positive thinking must be worked on daily. This is because people are emotionally led. We would like to believe that it is our intellect that leads us, but psychology teaches that we live by the 85/15 formula. This means that 85 percent of our decisions are based on feelings while only 15 percent are based on facts. We may use the facts to help justify a decision we have made, but we generally make these decisions for emotional reasons.

If you don't believe this, look around you. Why did you buy the clothes you're wearing? Any style would have been sufficient. How do you "feel" when you see a person you like or dislike? The things we choose to buy or feel are based on our emotions. The number of things you bought because you liked them probably exceeds the number of things you purchased out of sheer necessity.

Eventually you'll be able to control your feelings. It is at first an hour-by-hour, then a day-by-day choice. Once this is accomplished, you can come to terms with the past and no longer be enslaved by it. Your present life will now appear workable, and you will start to see small glimpses of a better future.

Your newly acquired healthy thoughts will serve you well. You will once again see new directions to go with your life. So many of the thoughts we become preoccupied with during grief are toxic. Toxic thoughts oppress you and keep you in unhealthy situations and relationships, whereas your newly recaptured healthy thoughts will empower you to pursue a better life.

As a minister, I (Mark) meet regularly with people who struggle with toxic thoughts. They often feel a need to confess these thoughts to me. They try to prepare me by telling me that they have a "bomb" to confess. I assure them that I can handle it. When they share this "bomb" and get no reaction from me, it always surprises them. As you move through the grief cycle day to day, you may have disturbing thoughts, but rest assured that others have wrestled with similar ones during their grief journey. We all have toxic thoughts because there really is nothing new under the sun. Yes, you are unique in how you put your thoughts together, but you are not unique in what those thoughts are.

Someone once said, "Thoughts are like birds: you cannot stop them from landing on your head, but you can stop them from building a nest there." A constructive way of dealing with negative thoughts is to admit you have them but refuse to be shocked by them. By doing this, you defuse any power they have over you. Once they're out in the open, they will not appear so sinister. How do you defuse these negative thoughts? You do it by exploring the possible reasons you're having them and then deciding to disregard them.

For quite a while after Jerry died, I (Kathy) lived with many toxic thoughts and very few boundaries. I believed I had been abandoned by everything important to me. I was uncertain and afraid. With all this going on inside me, I could not begin to heal. During this time, I received some very unhealthy advice from someone. She said, "You have got to stop crying so much, or no one is going to want to be around you." This was only six weeks after Jerry's death. I could not stop crying and because I had no boundaries I could not tell her to back off. Her "advice" made me feel very guilty. If I'd had healthy boundaries, I would have been able to disregard her advice and do my "grief work."

This was probably the most selfish time of my life. Was I totally self-centered? You bet I was! Did I have a choice? No, I didn't. I was too weak to make any choices at that point. I felt as though I was falling down a well, alone. When you have to force yourself to just get through the minutes in the day, it's impossible to be thoughtful of others too. You desperately need people, yet often all you do is take from them.

Because I had so few boundaries, I could not practice self-restraint. I was like a sponge who just soaked the life out of those around me. I needed healthy boundaries in order to get my life back on track. A positive response phase in the grief cycle? I didn't even know what those words meant then.

I (Mark) know exactly when I crossed over into the positive response. It was when I realized I had the ability to finally make the choice to live again. You have to wait until you have the strength to make this choice. When I realized that Sherry would always be a part of me, I knew I could continue to live. I had been afraid up to that point to close the final gap of the grief cycle. I thought that if I did, I would have to abandon memories of my wife. Of course that is not what it means at all. My wife was going to be part of me forever, so I could take my memories of her and of our love and get on with my life. I knew I could continue to live without guilt as well as without grief.

It took me a little more than three years to reconcile myself to my grief, although I had been told that it would take about a year. I found that at the end of that first year nothing was different. The same was true at the end of the second year, although I did sense a subtle change beginning. It was during the third year that it happened: I reconciled myself to the grief. I use the word *reconcile* because I believe you never completely get over the grief, but instead recognize and accept the reality and finality of it.

I had Sherry's name and her favorite flower tattooed on my chest. One day someone saw it and made the comment, "You'll have to live with that for the rest of your life." The ironic thing was, that was exactly the reason I had gotten the tattoo. Whether I married again or not, Sherry would always be part of me, in my heart and in my head.

Sherry and I were "one." We were soul mates in the way we thought, believed, and lived by faith. To know me was to know Sherry. A second spouse was going to have to understand that we would never share the same type of love as I had shared with Sherry. We could develop a very good marriage, but we would never have the oneness of my first marriage or its innocence. I wondered if I would ever find a woman who could accept that. Every time she would see me without a shirt on it would be a reminder that not only was Sherry's name tattooed on my chest, but she was also down inside my heart.

Whereas Mark knew exactly when he crossed over into the positive response of grief, I (Kathy) have no idea when it occurred for me, because I only realized it after the fact. Four years after Jerry died, Mark's father was visiting us. He is also a minister and was praying for people in our church. I asked him to pray that the past would assume its rightful place in my life. At that point, I still hurt so much, and I wanted it to stop; dare I say I wanted to feel better? I was experiencing the positive response phase of the grief cycle, but not with any regularity. It had been four very long years, and I was not progressing as I had hoped I would.

The following May my daughter Rachel was graduating from college. I wanted to give her something very special to mark the occasion. She didn't have many keepsakes from her father, so I took Jerry's and my wedding rings and had them melted down and made into a necklace for her. When I brought the necklace home, I tried it on to see how it looked. As I gazed at myself in the mirror, I thought: *This jewelry is from my past and that's where it belongs, not in my present.* I was wearing something that I really felt belonged to Rachel, not me. In that moment I knew that I had made the transition and had brought my grief to reconciliation. The past was where it belonged. My prayers really had been answered. Why is it that some of life's biggest transitions are only realized after the fact? I don't have an answer for that; I only know it was true in this case.

How did that make me feel? Very strange! I cried a little, but they were tears of relief; I was finally at peace with the past and what had been so overpowering and frightening just a few years before. I finally realized that putting things in the past really meant only putting the pain there. Jerry was still with me, but not painfully anymore. He was in death what he had been to me in life, a soothing presence.

A friend used to ask me after Jerry died if I would have become involved with him if I'd known he was going to die so young. She asked me if our relationship had been worth the pain his death caused me. I hated that question because, to be truthful, half the time I was not sure what the real answer was. But now, with the new realization that I had finally brought my grief to reconciliation, I knew the answer! Yes, most definitely it had been worth it. I knew I was a better person because of knowing Jerry and because of the painful lessons his death taught me. They say that everything you experience has the ability to positively transform you if you let it. I know with certainty that the experience I had with Jerry, and with surviving his death, has done just that for me. Grief has taught me many lessons.

63

Making the conscious decision to accept what has happened, to reconcile yourself to the grief, gives "conscious purpose" to your life. You are taking responsibility for the recovery you desire. You have now come to terms with your past and are no longer enslaved by it. Your present life is now workable and the future starts to give you glimpses that suggest things just might continue to get better.

I (Mark) remember stepping out onto my porch one morning and smelling the new day. I thought, *I want to live again.* A few months later, while outside on a stormy night watching the wind blow and tree limbs break, I shouted, "I really do want to live again." It felt so good to be thinking that. I would not have believed just three years before that I could ever feel that way again, but I did.

When we got married we even found wedding rings that perfectly symbolized our unique situation. They're called mountain rings. They are silver bands with a gold mountain range design on them. To us, the mountains and valleys represented the high and low points of our life experiences, both separately and together. We realized that every mountain, or high point, sat between two valleys, or low points. To us that meant that even though we had experienced such hard times there had still been good times along the way too.

Just recently we realized that there is another way we can look at the symbolism of our rings. We now choose to see that just one valley, or low point, sits between two mountains, or high points. We were so amazed! We had never looked at the rings that way before. When we saw that, we realized just how far we had come in being able to think positively. What a different perspective we are now using to look at life.

7

Stupid Things Good People Say

A wise comment concerning grief was used by Doug Manning as the title for his book *Don't Take My Grief Away*. He had heard a lady who was tormented and sorrowful say this to a person who was attempting to make her stop grieving. When Manning heard her say that, he wondered how many times he had tried to take the pain of grief away from people. He wondered how many times he had attempted to fill the air with philosophical statements, how many times he had bought into the fallacy that sympathy was somehow harmful. He wondered how many times he had robbed people of their grief in his efforts to avoid it.

You need to grieve in your own time and in your own way. You must work through the phases of grief, so they won't return later to haunt and harm you emotionally or physically. Don't let people rob you of what is a normal and healthy process. Grief is not an enemy to be avoided. For good mental health, you must go through the grief process. When you are in grief, your mind is overloaded. At times it feels ready to short-circuit. Try not to concern yourself with others' opinions. You and your immediate family are the only ones whom this death will permanently change. Other people's lives will return to normal; yours will never be "normal" again.

People who know you will look at your situation and feel pity for you. Even though they really care, they don't understand your situation. Experiencing a death, divorce, suicide, or incarceration makes you different. You fear that you are the topic of everyone's discussions and this further magnifies your loss. You feel exposed, and defenseless.

There will also be those who will judge you. They will see where you are—totally wounded and in deep grief—but they will judge you from where they are—mentally stable and living in comfortable security. This security has ceased to exist for you right now, and they don't understand that. They have no idea of the enormity of your loss or its devastating effect on you. They attempt to placate you with platitudes.

Platitudes are "one-size-fits-all" comments such as "God must have needed her in heaven more than you need her here" or "Things will be better soon, you just wait and see." Usually, people who offer platitudes are genuinely good people who really want to help. They have no idea that a hug or a meaningful look would be a much better way to express their condolences.

Unknowingly, they trivialize your grief. Platitudes suggest that your pain can be easily dealt with if you will just let it. Nothing could be further from the truth. Countless times we have heard recently bereaved people say, "I had no idea it would hurt this much." They've joined a club no one wants to belong to. The initiation into this club is the realization that this is a pain unlike any other. No one really understands it without experiencing it.

When we work with people in grief, the conversation always turns to the outrageous things they have heard from well-meaning people. The following platitudes and trivializations were spoken as words of comfort.

1. Vanessa had lost her father eleven months earlier. As Christmas approached, she was asked if she was ready for the holiday. She replied that she was not really in the Christmas spirit. She confided that she was depressed over her father not being there to share in the festivities. The person she was talking to then said, "Are you still upset over that? You should stop being so self-centered and get in the spirit for your niece and nephew."

2. Eileen's first husband died, and shortly thereafter her mother died too. A few years later she was facing the impending death of her second husband. A friend commented to her, "After all you've been through, this death probably won't even bother you."

3. While out for ice cream one evening, after Kathy had broken her neck in a car accident and was wearing a neck brace, I (Mark) saw a man who had known Sherry and me. He looked at Kathy and asked what had happened. When I told him, he said, "Boy, you don't have much luck with wives, do you?"

4. A preschool boy was murdered. Soon after the police recovered his body, a relative said to the boy's mother, "I just know God has a blessing in this for you somewhere down the line."

5. While grieving the death of one of her twin babies, a mother was told, "Thank God you have the other baby to replace her."

6. A ten-year-old boy was told innumerable times at his father's wake, "Guess you're the man of the house now." Three months after his father's death he started having nightmares. When his mother finally got him to talk about what was bothering him, he reluctantly admitted that he didn't know where he was going to find a job that would support his family after he quit the fourth grade to go to work. He was consumed with guilt over it.

The prevailing question throughout is, how does one respond to these comments? The people making them really are trying to say the right thing. They just have no idea of the damage they're inflicting on the already damaged person.

There can be a common response when you are ambushed with a platitude that requires an answer. The perfect response is, "I'm working on it." This is such a nebulous statement and can mean so many things. It might mean, "I'm working on not putting my hands around your throat and choking the life out of you," or it can also mean, "You're right and I am trying." In any case, the objective here is to get you through the situation. Saying "I'm working on it" really accomplishes that.

I (Kathy) had a trivializing experience when I had a car accident. I collided head-on with a man driving a truck who had passed a car on a double solid line. We were both traveling at 60 mph. My injury was misdiagnosed at the hospital. They thought I had just sprained my neck, when in reality I had broken it. I was sent home and spent two and a half weeks getting sick to my stomach, experiencing dizzy spells and having the sensation of light bulbs popping in my eyes. At another hospital, I was correctly diagnosed with a severed C5 vertebra.

When the surgeon examined me, he couldn't believe I had survived the accident or that I had walked around with a completely broken neck for two weeks. He frankly explained that he wasn't sure he could successfully correct this problem, and if he was unable to, I would wake up paralyzed. I had to go through an entire night unsure of what the outcome would be—complete recovery or complete paralysis. It was a total nightmare for Mark too, especially since Sherry had died of a broken neck. The surgery, thank God, was 100 percent successful. There are no words to adequately express how thankful both Mark and I were. It was, however, a lot to cope with—nearly dying, knowing I probably should have died, walking around with a broken neck (which is impossible, but yet true in my case) and then coming through the surgery successfully. I needed time to come to terms with all of this.

The day after my surgery I started receiving humorous cards from very caring people who were only trying to lift my spirits. The cards did little to cheer me. Instead, they made me angry. I was very confused and ashamed over my anger at this outpouring of concern. It was later that I learned the source of my anger came from feeling trivialized. To me, this was no time for jokes. The experience was as bad for me as losing Jerry had been. I was incapable of making light of it.

I (Mark) work as a chaplain for Hospice. Right after I first learned how we all unthinkingly trivialize people at times, I was assigned to visit Rose. She was 90 years old and suffering from cancer. She was very lively and talkative. We quickly developed a good relationship and she felt comfortable confiding in me. One day Rose was feeling depressed. The cancer, which was concentrated in her leg, had caused tremendous swelling. She confided that she was ashamed of her body. I started to reassure her by saying, "Now Rose, you look just fine, don't you feel that way," and then I remembered what I had learned about trivializing. Instead I responded with, "It must be so uncomfortable for you and even embarrassing."

I could see Rose's whole demeanor change. It is so true that you help people best when you reach them where they are. You cannot do that until you really listen. When we want to feel understood, we always search out that special pair of ears. They belong to people we know will listen to us without judging. It's hard sometimes to find those ears. When Rose felt understood, she was able to move on and talk about other things.

When platitudes and trivializations are spoken it is always with the best of intentions. Ninety days after Sherry died, people expected me (Mark) to start living again in a normal fashion. They told me I should be dating, looking for another wife. These were things I absolutely could not do, and I couldn't believe people were advising me to do them. These were "spiritual" people, too, my mentors—people who claimed they were hearing God. They were not! I was still in shock, and the agony of grief was coming. Hell was coming. I was still numb, not believing what had happened. I still believed this situation might actually go away, that it might just be a bad test or dream that would somehow end. I felt trivialized by their good intentions.

Most people don't even notice that others around them are hurting. They couldn't notice because so much of the pain is on the inside. These are caring people who want to do anything they can to ease your pain. However, when you're in grief, you can become oversensitive and hear criticism where none is intended. Before you judge these people too harshly, ask yourself—did you know before you experienced the death of your loved one just how deep the pain would go, how long it would hurt, how misunderstood you would feel? If you're truthful, you will have to admit that you didn't, so don't be so quick to judge those who are just trying to help you. They trivialize only because they don't understand what you're going through. They can't understand because they are not where you are. Look them right in the eye after they utter a platitude that doesn't help a bit, but requires an answer, and say "I'm working on it."

So what _should_ someone say to a grieving person? Our advice is to use comments like "I can't imagine what you are going through right now" or "This has to be so hard for you, I'm so sorry." These are not only appropriate but fit most devastating situations. They effectively express what you really mean, and they don't rob the grieving person of his pain. You have connected with him where he is. You have touched him at his level instead of trying to drag him up to yours. There _is_ power in your words. They can reinforce and validate a person, or have the opposite effect.

Author Norman Cousins describes a situation he witnessed that convinced him that life and death are in the power of our words.

A critically ill patient had suffered a massive heart attack. His cardiac muscle function was irreparably compromised. The doctors verbally agreed in front of him that he had "a wholesome, very loud third-sound gallop."[1] This meant that the heart muscle was straining and failing. However, this patient slowly and unexpectedly improved, and eventually was discharged from the hospital. Months later, when asked about his remarkable recovery, the man said he knew he was going to be all right when he heard the doctors say he had a "wholesome gallop." He figured it meant that he still had a lot of kick left in his heart, and that he was going to be healthy. He was supposed to die, but believed what he had misunderstood.

We respond according to our faith, be it true or not. Faith is what causes us to build our internal reality, which is the way we see things and what we hope for.

For those who may look back and feel a little guilty because of the platitudes they may have uttered in the past, we say the same thing to you that we say to people who regret something they did while grieving: you did the best you could at the time. That's all anyone can expect of you.

8

Friends

There are three kinds of people in the world: those who are for you, those who are against you, and those who don't care at all. It's not that these people are cold and thoughtless. It's just that your grief is not part of their life. This is hard to understand, because your world has stopped while theirs has continued unabated. It is difficult sometimes to discern which kind of person you're encountering. Rest assured, however, that you'll find out soon, probably in a few short months.

Your most helpful friend will be the good listener who is nonjudgmental and accepting. He will be able to hear the good as well as the bad without judging you. He will believe in you, and will endure the long time needed for recovery after all others seem to have forgotten you. Most of all, he will not fail you. You will find out during this time what you need and value most in a friend.

The true friend I (Mark) had was Charlie. He was there for me even when I didn't know I needed help. He listened to my anger, hurt, and frustration. He cried as well as laughed with me. He shared good memories with me and was there long hours. Yet he would give me time alone. He kept everything entrusted to him in confidence. He was my friend.

However, all relationships change—some for better, some for worse. Discomfort in the presence of a friend can indicate a lack of acceptance. Just as you realize you're now a different person because of circumstances beyond your control, you also must accept the fact that you now have different needs. This means you have to reevaluate friendships and decide which ones are no longer viable for your life. With some people, you may decide you need to be friends from a distance.

The next time you feel uneasy about being with an old friend, ask yourself if that friend is accepting you for who you are now. Is he is giving you the affirmation and acceptance you need? If not, be thankful for the good times you shared but move on to relationships that mutually give and receive understanding and respect. These two things are the bedrock of a friendship.

Doug Manning, in *Don't Take My Grief Away*, says:

> The unhelpful listener will say that talking doesn't do any good, counsels not to be weak (i.e., express too much pain or sadness), urges you to think of others who are worse off, sees the female's expression of anger as unladylike, frightening or sexually unattractive. Will see the male's expression of sadness, longing, or despair as being unmanly, a waste of time, an indication of impending collapse and will urge you to focus on tomorrow and forget the past.[2]

Friends are often at a loss for words when they're with you because (and don't forget this) they have suffered a loss too. When they don't know what to say to you, it isn't because they don't care. It's often because they are so overcome with emotion themselves.

The first time I (Kathy) went out in public after Jerry's death, I encountered a close friend who, before she could stop herself, blurted out, "I haven't been to see you because I can't bear to look at you. You make me feel so bad." I could tell by the look on her face that she couldn't believe she had just said that. To make it worse, for her, she kept on talking, digging herself into a deeper hole of embarrassment. She got away from me as soon as she could. I knew she had meant well, but I commented to my son, "Maybe I should just wear a bag over my head to make it easier for people to avoid me."

Friends feel so helpless at this time. They think saying "I'm sorry" is not enough. It sounds so inadequate and they want to say something profound. They don't understand that words won't ease your pain. However, because they are your friends, they keep on trying.

Here are five suggestions for helping a friend in grief, from Susan McClelland's _If There's Anything I Can Do:_

1. If you are going to speak your sorry-ness, keep your statement simple. The goal is to get to the point where you can handle "I'm sorry" in such a way that the friend you have spoken to does not have to talk about _it_.
2. Show how you feel by putting your arms around your troubled friend. This is a powerful antidote to misery.
3. Beware of gossip. Personal misfortunes, unlike illness or injury, bring about a whole web of unverified rumor, half-truths and innuendoes.
4. Be prepared for failure. Go ahead and assume that your friend will respond brusquely. It can happen.

5. Stay in touch, whatever the response to "I'm sorry." Days from now, when too many friends drift away, figuring the "worst is over," your reminders that you have not forgotten can be a big help. The "worst" can be a long, lonely road.[3]

An alternative to saying something is to write a note to the bereaved person. Jerry died in mid-June, and at the end of August I (Kathy) received a note from one of his co-workers. She apologized for waiting so long to get in touch, and wrote the most poignant letter. Receiving her letter at that particular time was such a comfort to me. By then, two months later, I thought everyone had forgotten Jerry. That letter was just what I needed to reassure me that although people had resumed their lives, they had not forgotten Jerry or us. The advantage of a note over a phone call is that it can be read over and over.

About a month after Jerry's death I (Mark) wrote Kathy a note that simply stated that I knew from experience what she was going through, and I wanted her to know that my family and I were praying for her. I told her that I had not known Jerry more than to say hello, but since we both lived in the same neighborhood I could tell by observation that they were a close family. I asked her to call me if there was anything I could do—from sharing what I experienced with the death of my wife and learning about the grief cycle to using my swimming pool. I told her not to feel odd asking, as I was just down the street from her.

That note really touched me (Kathy). Although we had never met, here was a person who had been where I was now. At my most desperate, I reached out, and Mark offered me friendship. He listened and reinforced what I was saying by simple nods of his head. He commiserated with me by sharing his experience with grief. By doing that, I knew he understood what I was going through.

You may be surprised that some people, whom you assumed would stick by you will distance themselves, while others who were not formerly close will be there for you. You may have no clue why people you considered close friends are now withdrawing. There is a mourning in that too.

If I (Kathy) had been told before Jerry died that people I considered close friends were going to distance themselves from me, I would have flatly refused to believe it. The saddest part of the whole thing was that at age 40, I couldn't go up to people and ask them, "Why don't you like me anymore?" They probably wouldn't have told me—or worse yet, they might have. Either way, I wasn't strong enough to hear their answer.

For example, when Mark and I married, I invited Jerry's college roommate and his wife to the wedding. Jerry and I had maintained a friendship with this couple throughout our marriage. They had both been very good to me in the early days of my grief. However, they didn't come to the wedding. I heard afterward, through a mutual friend, that they thought their presence would remind me too much of Jerry, and would ruin the day for me. Reminders of Jerry weren't hurtful, but their not coming to the wedding was.

With death, you feel rejection from many sides and it just tears you up, leaving you feeling isolated and empty. Rejection does this to you because people are created to have relationships. Relationships give us our identity, security, acceptance, and significance. You have to eventually accept this rejection, as hard as that is, and then move on to life-ministering relationships with people who will accept you as you are. The way to test whether you have accepted the monster of rejection and moved on is to ask yourself if you are bitter. Bitterness blinds you, lies to you, and can destroy you. If you do not admit to any bitterness issues and rid yourself of them, they can adversely affect all your relationships.

I (Kathy) dealt with varying degrees of bitterness for about four years after Jerry died, and it definitely had an effect on me. My self-confidence was very low. I would do things like walk into a store and look around, and if I spotted someone I knew I would walk the other way or leave the store completely. I just didn't want to face anyone and perhaps be rejected. No matter if you are an adult or a child, the feeling of rejection leaves you empty. As long as you feel this way, it is impossible to form a sound structure to rebuild your life and once again give it meaning.

One day I walked into a store and didn't stop at the door to scan the place for people I might know. If I did meet up with someone, I now possessed enough self-confidence and knew I could handle it. That's when I realized I had moved on. I had replaced the people I felt rejected by with people who accepted me for who I was and liked me anyway. The bitterness was gone.

I also realized that most people I felt rejected by were really Jerry's friends originally. He had been the link between them and me. When he died, the relationships with them naturally died too. What we had once had in common had ceased to exist, so the relationships eventually ceased to exist also. It was a tremendous relief when I finally figured that out. I could finally forgive those people and remember, without bitterness, the good times Jerry and I had shared with them. This realization also helped restore my self confidence.

An added bonus was that I developed a deeper appreciation for those who had stuck with me, as well as new friends I had made. These people allowed me to grieve by doing the most important thing a friend can do, listening to me. This is what a real friend does. He listens. As the survivor of a death, you may need to verbalize the details of the experience repeatedly. By doing this, you're attempting to make sense of the whole thing. No matter how many times he has heard it, the wise and loving friend will listen, agree, and give you needed understanding.

Barb was that kind friend to me (Kathy) during this time. I would say to her, "Stop me if I've told you this before," and even though she had heard the same thing many times, she would still listen as though she were hearing it for the first time. This kind of friend will be a life preserver for you.

A friend will offer advice, not give well-meaning orders. As a bereaved person, you need to guard against becoming overly sensitive to your friend's advice or comments. Try your best not to hear criticism where none is intended. A grieving person often does this. Your friend needs to be aware of this so he can be patient. He needs to realize, for his own sanity, that you may not be an easy person to love at this time.

There are four fundamental guidelines for helping someone in grief:

1. Don't withdraw from the survivor, stay available. Be that special ear that is so important for the bereaved person to have.
2. Don't compare, evaluate, or judge.
3. Don't expect sympathy for yourself.
4. Don't patronize the bereaved person.[4]

At the risk of repeating ourselves, we cannot emphasize enough the ignorance of well-meaning friends who violate the first two guidelines. They often will withdraw. The real friend needs to guard against doing this.

Real friends offer help and will be there when needed. Take them up on their offers of assistance. I (Kathy) found when I broke my neck in the car accident that people really did mean it when they offered help. A friend in our church organized people to bring us meals. Several of these people told me that they found it so gratifying to be able to help in a way that was genuinely needed. If people found it an inconvenience to help you, they would not offer their services. Those who helped me felt encouraged by giving me encouragement. Think of it this way: if your best friend were in need, would you want him to reach out to you? Since you know the answer is yes, why would you think your friends are any different when you're in need?

If you're a friend of a bereaved person, remember that he is going through the most painful, confusing time of his life. Have consideration for him and let him work through it in his own way and in his own time. Just being available and listening will often be the most effective, appreciated thing you can do.

9

The Myths of Grief

The myths that surround grief make it harder to cope with. We are a death-denying society. We attempt to ignore any problem we can't solve. When something unpleasant happens, we try to gloss over it so we can quickly put it behind us and move on to something more pleasant.

We gloss over it by creating myths about it. We buy into these myths until we are faced with the death of a loved one. Then we are forced to confront reality and battle the myths. We find out they are not true. The following are some of the most common myths about grief as Alan Woefelt[5] and Therese Rando see them.

1. **Asking what happened and talking about the deceased will increase the pain of the bereaved.** On the contrary, telling the story over and over and talking about the deceased are the most important elements for grief recovery.

2. **Most people want to grieve alone.** Most people need and want the support of family and friends who will listen and not try to rescue them from their pain.

3. **People can be replaced.** Each person is unique and cannot be replaced. Having a baby will not replace a child who has died.

4. **Normal grief takes about one year.** It can take anywhere from three to five years, depending on the intensity and duration of the relationship, the type of death, and the social support system.

5. **It's strange for the bereaved to laugh.** It is no disrespect to the dead to laugh. The bereaved shouldn't grieve all the time.

6. **You are bothering a bereaved person by calling to see how he is, especially on anniversaries and holidays.** You are *not* bothering him. He feels very alone on these days, and knowing someone is thinking about him is of tremendous help.

7. **The grieving person is having major trouble if he thinks he hears or sees the deceased.** This is a very common occurrence, and shouldn't be viewed as mental impairment if it happens.

8. **You never get over the pain of the loss.** Remembering without pain is the goal of grief recovery. It is achievable—eventually.

9. **All losses are the same.** When you grieve for your parent, you're grieving your past; when you grieve for your child, you're grieving your future; and when you grieve for your spouse, you are grieving your present. Not all losses are the same.

10. **All bereaved people grieve in the same way.** Just as people are unique in the way they live their lives, they're also unique in the way they grieve. For example, some people cannot sleep at all when they are in the throes of heavy grief, while others find that all they do is sleep. Differences are what make the world go around.

11. **When grief is resolved, it never comes up again.** Based on our experiences with our own grief, as well as helping others through theirs, we doubt that anyone ever "gets over" grief. Reconciliation is a more accurate concept. You accept that your loved one is gone, and the pain of this knowledge does diminish, but you never really close the chapter on grief in your life.

12. **Death is death—there no difference between sudden and anticipated death.** Imagine a person walking down the street. He sees someone running toward him with a knife. He knows he's going to get stabbed, so he's able to brace himself for it. This is what anticipated death is like. Another person is walking down the street and is stabbed in the back. He didn't see it coming. He had no time to brace himself for it. This is what sudden death is like. Now

who hurts more? They both do. Each person's grief is unique, though—because each set of circumstances is unique.

When, in your grief, you fail to live up to these myths, you may feel guilty. This guilt is then complicated by a society that has bought into these myths. They sit in judgment of you.

I (Kathy) am ashamed to admit that I have personal experience with myth number six. After my father died, and my mother was in Florida on his birthday, I didn't call her. I figured she was probably having a relaxing time and would not be thinking about his birthday. I figured wrong, but didn't realized it until my own bereavement.

So, beware of myths. They can really wound you if you're in grief. They can also bring tremendous guilt to friends who are trying to comfort you. They find out later that their good intentions only served to add to your pain. They were only doing what "everyone" said was the best thing to help. It seemed like the natural thing to do, but grief is not a natural situation. Your life is no longer filled with hope. You need extra sensitivity and thoughtfulness.

When a friend asks, "What can I do?" you may respond, "I don't know." Your friend will typically say, "Well, give me a call if you do need anything." The problem is that you're too overwhelmed to make that call, so you don't get any help. You become convinced that no one cares. The sad reality is that there has simply been miscommunication and misunderstanding from all sides.

10

Children

Our children's responses to the news of the deaths and the aftermath will forever remain with us. We both agree that nothing will ever be as hard as breaking that news to ones so young and innocent.

I (Mark) will never forget my daughters walking into the living room the morning after their mother was killed and standing there in their pajamas, knowing something was terribly wrong but too afraid to ask. Taking them upstairs to their bedroom and telling them about their mother's death was the hardest thing I have ever done in my life. After that experience, life's problems now seem rather insignificant. Overpopulation, global warming, another Great Depression, the bomb, or even Armageddon—so what? Please don't waste our time. The breaking of our children's hearts broke ours even more.

Children learn a lot about loss from TV, movies, and books. Unfortunately, those sources are full of misinformation. For example, a character on TV is nearly killed during a show, but by the end of the program he's alive and well with barely a scratch on him. This cannot help but give children a false reality about life, not to mention death. Death shatters a child's perception that the world is a safe place.

How do we prepare them for this? The best way is to maintain open communication from the time the child is very young. When your child feels free to discuss most anything with you, chances are you can talk and help him cope if a death occurs.

Watch for a window of opportunity—a very tiny amount of time that pops up unexpectedly when your child decides he wants to talk. This may happen while you're cooking dinner, washing the dishes, or watching TV. The key is to stop whatever you're doing when the child broaches the subject of the deceased, sit down, and talk. Keep your answers to your child's questions simple and truthful. Don't assume or put words in his mouth. Ask questions for clarification, and encourage your child to express his feelings. Sometimes this is hard for him to do. He may be afraid his true feelings will hurt you and he knows you have been hurt enough. Reassure him that you want to hear what's on his mind.

Probably the most important thing for you to remember as you help your child deal with his grief is that you are the role model. If you hide your grief, your child will too. A counselor related how a mother and her three children came to him for counseling after the death of her husband. He interviewed the mother separately from her children. He asked her when she chose to grieve over her husband's death and she replied that she waited until the children were all in bed at night. She did not want to upset them by letting them see her cry.

He then interviewed the children and asked them when they grieved for their father. They replied that they always waited until they were in bed, so they wouldn't upset their mother with their crying. How sad that this loving, thoughtful family, who should have been sharing their grief in order to divide their pain, were forcing themselves to hide that pain from each other.

An excellent way to generate discussions on grief with your child is to read age-appropriate books with him that relate to death. After reading the book, you can each share your feelings about the information. You can recap each chapter and see if it generates any discussion. Engaging in play activities is also an excellent way to encourage your child to express his feelings.

Inviting your child to visit the gravesite is another way to engage him in the grief process. However, don't put pressure on him to do this if he doesn't feel comfortable with it. Remember, working through grief is an individual process.

If you are dealing with a child in adolescence, you need to realize that adolescents have their hands full just trying to find their own identities in life. They usually have an adultlike understanding of the irreversibility of the death by this age. They probably view death as the enemy, but at the same time may appear fascinated by it. They often will need verbal permission to grieve, and their anger may be either passive or aggressive.

Children under twelve often grieve through the games they play. They may take a backseat in their peer interaction, and their grades may take a drastic nose dive for a while.

If children are old enough to love, then they're old enough to grieve. Children will also grieve in doses. At times they may seem emotionless. This is a very normal defense mechanism.

Losing a loved one rips away the love and security a child needs. This further complicates the child's quest for identity. The intense grief, which usually lasts approximately a year, is sometimes extended for the adolescent. Karen Gravelle writes in *Teenagers Face to Face with Bereavement,* "It's usually about a year before you can talk about it. Because before you can tell people about it, you have to accept it. And it takes a while for that."[6] She goes on to say:

> As reality focuses, the initial denial, shock and depression give way, exposing a range of agonizing and often conflicting feelings. Added to the usual intense and confusing emotions typical of adolescence, the pain, anger, and guilt of bereavement present grieving teenagers with a lot to handle.[7]

This concept could be compared to dumping a truckload of weight onto a mini-car and expecting it to hold up. It is just not made to handle that much of a load, just as the child is not created to handle such devastation. Guilt and regret are expressed in comments like, "I didn't get a chance to say good-bye" or "I should have done...."

The worst thing for my (Kathy's) daughter Rachel was knowing that the last thing she ever said to her father was "I hate you" when she talked to him on the phone an hour before he died. They'd had some minor disagreement that at age fourteen she had blown out of proportion. This memory continued to haunt her for about five years. As she matured, she realized that things like this just happen, and when they do, you often get no second chances to correct them.

She finally confronted this issue one night after having too much to drink. She was literally trying to drown her sorrows over her guilt. It was painful to watch, but at least she finally faced it. Once she could truthfully discuss how bad she felt, she could finally put it behind her. The wall of guilt came down. She and I were able to finally talk about the whole episode. She was able to look at it from a more adult perspective. She could finally accept that fourteen-year-olds often react without thinking and say things that would be better left unsaid. After much lengthy discussion, she was able to let it go.

Having guilty thoughts and destructive feelings, i.e., suicidal thoughts, is natural. It's important to recognize and accept them as being all right to examine. These feelings are not something to be ashamed of. Encourage the child to share these thoughts too.

Often, in addition to shame, a child may feel unworthy, unlovable, mortified or humiliated. He will often exaggerate his inadequacies by going to extremes in the negative response phase of the grief cycle. The core problem is hurt disguised as rebellion. The child is actually crying out for help, understanding and security.

It's unfair for a child to feel shame over the death, but this is so often the case. The child is embarrassed over losing. Whenever you feel you have lost, it's an embarrassment. You expect to be successful. The death leaves the child feeling like a failure.

In _The Grieving Child,_ Helen Fitzgerald writes that after a death, parents tend to let the daily routines of life slide. The best thing for the child, however, is to keep as much of the same routine in place as possible—because routine equals security to the child. It gives the child's life predictability. Discipline should also be enforced as much as possible. The child badly needs to know that someone is still in charge.

Returning to school as soon after the death as possible will also help the child regain security. It's a good idea to discuss with the child how the people at school should be told about the death. Children sometimes have very definite ideas about how they want things handled. Ask the child's teacher to speak to the class before the child returns.

The teacher might want to ask the class for suggestions on how best to help your child cope. Making the class part of the solution helps them take ownership for making your child feel comfortable upon returning to school. The teacher could even help the children rehearse what to say to your child when he first returns to the classroom. All these precautions can help to ease your child's embarrassment at what has happened.

The first Sunday back at church, after the funeral, I (Mark) remember my youngest daughter, Elisabeth, standing outside the door of the church and telling me, "I don't want to go in." At that time I didn't understand her thinking pattern, but I knew she needed encouragement. I know now she was simply embarrassed to face others.

Claudia Jewett equates the child's soul to a bucket and says:

> When a child loses or changes caretakers (parents), the bucket is "sloshed" and some of these good feelings about self and others are spilled. If the child has strong feelings of guilt and shame, he develops "leaks" in his bucket. He may shrug off positive strokes. The resulting depletion makes the child needy, demanding and reluctant or unable to give back much to anyone.[8]

Many times parents, or those in authority, are inadvertently responsible for emptying the child's bucket. Adults need to constantly be on guard against negative exchanges with the child. Negative interaction depletes so many of the good feelings the child needs during the time of recovery. Any negative behaviors need to be addressed, but in a positive way.

The child's identity is based on his parent's acceptance. His needs are met through communicated love and this acceptance. The death of a parent creates a state of emptiness. The child wants to love and be loved by the deceased. Suddenly nothing seems concrete to the child. The emptiness seems to suck the life from him. Love makes a person, and without that love, you feel like nothing, be you adult or child.

11

Slow Healing

It took me (Kathy) five very long years to reconcile my self to the loss of Jerry. After three years, I still felt I was dying on the inside much of the time. I was wondering more and more—was I really in grief, or had it just turned into self-pity? I would often think how normal I appeared to others. I knew that if they could just look beneath my calm exterior, they would see I was desperately sorrowful much of the time. I felt I was performing a role each day. The weird thing was that no one suspected. I began to worry: would I forevermore appear calm and sane outwardly but be very much something else inwardly?

Mark called my condition "normal abnormality." Was it abnormal to be two people in one? Yes it was, but I was in an abnormal situation: grief. The loss of a loved one can send you into deep despair and withdrawal, with long periods of crying, insomnia, and suicidal feelings. These behaviors are abnormal, but quite common during grief.

Distorted and mythical thinking is another frequent byproduct of grief. Negatives about the deceased tend to get pushed aside, and only the positives are remembered. It seems that the best way to make a "saint" of someone is to have them die.

Suicidal thoughts are another normal abnormality. Grieving people think of suicide as a way to stop hurting. If a bereaved person broaches the topic of suicide, don't take it lightly. Don't respond with shock, anger, or denunciation, but instead with love, concern, and understanding. Seek professional help promptly if the person seems to be preparing to attempt suicide, or talks about it frequently.

Suicidal thoughts are just one indication of complicated mourning. Some other signs are persistent fear, prolonged physical complaints without any organic findings, prolonged feelings of guilt, chronic patterns of apathy and/or depression, consistent withdrawal from friends or family members, dramatic changes in sleeping and eating patterns, and drug or alcohol abuse. Any such pattern that persists over a prolonged period of time requires attention, and may call for professional help.

Some normal, uncomplicated mourning signs are sadness, anger, guilt, self-reproach, anxiety, loneliness, fatigue, helplessness, shock, yearning for the lost person, and numbness. These could be accompanied by a number of physical symptoms, ranging from tightness in the chest to inability to watch TV to having very lifelike dreams. Beyond this, you may find yourself preoccupied with thoughts of disbelief, like *I know I'm going to wake up and this will be over.* You may think you hear your loved one say your name, or smell his or her presence.

Mark and I married just eight months after Jerry's death. Ironically, my mother and children were the biggest supporters of the marriage. My mother, having been widowed herself, knew the despair I was experiencing. My children knew my heart was broken. They felt that if there was someone who could bring me happiness and comfort, then I should go ahead and make a life with him. As my daughter Rachel said, it was not as though Jerry and I had divorced and there was a chance we would get back together. He had died, and I was forced to live. I had been given no choice in the matter.

However, not everyone I knew was as understanding. Some people were very shocked. They wondered how I could do this so soon. One person actually asked me what I would do if Jerry came back. How do you answer a question like that? People seemed to think I had "gotten stupid" once Jerry was no longer here and it was their duty to ask me questions like, "Have you really given this enough thought?" A part of me wanted to say "Well goooollllly, no I haven't. Thank you so very much for bringing it to my attention." In their eyes, I was not behaving rationally. I just had to keep in mind that this was their opinion, not mine.

There will always be those who are for you, and those who seem to be against you (who usually have no real understanding of what you're experiencing). Many of the people who were the most encouraging when I remarried were the ones who had gone through very hard times in their own lives.

There was so much people didn't know about my situation. Jerry was a wonderful man, my best friend, who thought I was the funniest person he ever knew. I could make him laugh so hard he would actually cry. We always had a good time together (no, I'm not making him out to be a saint here). A friend commented to me that she had seen us just before he died, and had thought to herself how evident it was that we were more than husband and wife, we were also good friends. She said she noticed it because it was something she rarely saw with most couples and she envied me that.

I also knew that what we had was not the norm in many of my peers' marriages. For example, if I was home from work for the day, he would call me from his office at least three or four times just to chat. It was things like this that made the void from his death so devastating.

Having been through the death of my wife, I (Mark) offered to talk to Kathy if she ever felt the need. On the lowest night of her widowhood, two months after the death, a friend insisted she call me. Her friend knew that Kathy needed more help than she, who had never experienced anything like this, was able to give her. I was able to offer the understanding of one who had walked in her shoes. I didn't give her any false hope or platitudes. I told her it wouldn't get better for a very long time. I didn't tell her that she would make it, as if it were a foregone conclusion and would just naturally happen. Instead I said she *could* make it if she chose. I told her it would be a hard-fought battle that would seem hopeless much of the time.

My being so brutally honest was a relief to her. I had not sugar-coated the truth, and ironically this was what gave her a flicker of hope. I was living proof for her that it was possible to go through this hell on earth and live to tell about it. We continued to meet to talk, and within a short time we grew close.

I saw the *real* her, and so did she—for perhaps the first time in her life. You also will find the real you during this harrowing time. It is a genuine learning process. Prepare yourself, because a lot of what you'll learn may be disheartening at first. On the other hand, you'll also discover strengths you never knew you possessed. You'll uncover personality traits that have never surfaced before, because they never needed to. You will seem to be transformed into a new person in many ways.

The real you may at first be composed of little more than weak desperation due to the tragedy you have been forced to endure. Some people will tell you how strong you are, but you'll know it's not strength they're seeing. It's merely a person who is not dead but not quite alive either. You will feel as if you can barely move, and you may be amazed as well as amused that someone views this as strength.

I (Kathy) had no capacity to put on any false airs. I was confused, sad beyond belief, and totally without hope. I remember sitting on my porch on the Fourth of July, less than a month after Jerry's death, and thinking to myself that nothing exciting or good would ever happen to me again. It was the worst feeling, to be so utterly without hope. I was afraid of everything, yet fearful of nothing, a walking oxymoron. Death no longer scared me, yet going to the grocery store did—now is that confusion or what?

My exasperation with myself often led to explosive behavior. But Mark understood all this. With his help, I realized that it was natural to be angry and that I had to find healthy outlets for it. He helped me deal with the shame I felt over feeling so angry so much of the time. He really understood me, but liked me anyway. It was because of his genuine understanding that I felt confident marrying him so soon after Jerry's death. When Jerry died, my ability to love did not die. My need to be needed still existed. For a while both got buried in grief, but they did resurface and wouldn't be denied. They didn't emerge because I wanted them to. In fact, that's the absolute last thing I wanted to happen. But they did resurface because they were part of who I was.

You may find yourself facing needs and feelings you wish would stay buried. However, if they are there, they won't just go away. The length of time it takes them to come forth is different for each person.

I had two children who needed male guidance, and here was a man who understood the entire situation. He wanted to make a life with me. The memory of Jerry, which loomed over everything, never threatened Mark. After grieving himself for so many years, he knew what I was going through. He was prepared for all of it. He even told me it was all right to pretend he was Jerry when we made love, if doing so gave me comfort (only a widowed person would understand this).

I have to make one thing perfectly clear at this point. Mark's love, support, and honesty didn't make the pain of my grief any less. Nothing could. The bad times were still intensely bad. The terrible waves of grief continued to haunt me for the next four years. I was so very thankful to have Mark. I always knew that he completely understood when I was in the throes of grief.

For example, I had nightmares regularly for two years after we got married. I would usually wake up crying, and it was an absolute godsend to have Mark there to calm me and talk me through it, even though he couldn't take it away. It is very true that misery loves company, and that's the role Mark played in my struggle with grief so much of the time.

No one, no drug, no drink will take away your grief. The hurt is far too painful, because it's inside you and it's all-consuming. It travels from your heart to your head and back again, and it replays itself in countless ways, countless times.

As you move toward reconciliation, it's important to understand that you'll never forget your loved one. There's no reason you should. As time goes on, your loved one will assume the proper place in your new life. Don't let yourself be convinced otherwise. On our honeymoon, we both realized that there would always be four of us in this marriage, because Jerry and Sherry would always be part of us. This was only right, since they had helped make us the people we were up to that point.

12

Suppose There
Were a Miracle

Solution-Oriented Brief Therapy is a counseling technique that is gaining wide recognition. The premise behind this therapy is that every problem has a solution. This solution can be discovered in a brief amount of time, and is generated by the client, not the counselor. This sort of counseling doesn't dwell on the problems. It focuses on helping people create solutions, or, as Insoo Kim Berg, a leader in the field of this therapy, says, "co-create" solutions.

Clients who learn to look through the lens of solution-focused therapy become filled with new possibilities for change. There is encouragement, hope, and fresh motivation. They move beyond mere insight, blame, and analysis. Couples discover how to solve problems mutually.

The therapist begins the first session by asking the "miracle question": "Just suppose you went to bed tonight and a miracle occurred. This miracle has made everything in your life perfect. No, your loved one didn't return, but other than that, things are perfect. How would others know, by observing your behavior, that this miracle has occurred in your life?"

I (Mark) posed this question to Joe, whom I was counseling. I asked him, "How would your family know that a miracle had taken place?" Joe replied, "I would sit down at the table and have breakfast with them. I would smile at them and make eye contact." I asked him how many mornings he would do this, and he told me, "Every morning." I knew he had to be more realistic about his goal. I asked him if he would attempt sitting at the breakfast table, smiling, and making eye contact with his family for just one week. He said he would. This may not sound like much, but with this type of therapy, "little is good." A week later Joe reported that his family really noticed these few small changes, and when he saw what a difference they made, he was eager to try further changes.

Grieving people often view life as one huge problem. If you can "just suppose there were a miracle," and then decide on one little thing to change, it might lead to an improvement in your life. What small thing can you think of to work on? Remember, little is good. Keep it simple. If it works, do more of it. If it doesn't work, do something different. Will this cure your grief? No, but some of your overwhelming problems could start to appear solvable. This will be most effective when your choices are very specific, realistic, detailed, and achievable. Only you know what that involves. By being realistic and specific, you are dealing with your inner feelings as well as the desired results.

Eileen, a member of one of our support groups, said that if there were a miracle, people would know because she would stand up straight, throw her shoulders back, and look straight ahead when she walked. The very first time she did this, one of her family members commented, "You look different, you look pretty!" It made her day.

Setting a small goal and actually reaching it feels so gratifying when you are in grief. Because of what you've recently been through, you may think you can't reach any goals. You might hesitate to set any. You also might be unable to think of any goals to set. That is why the emphasis here is on setting small goals. They are easier to formulate and reach. To aid you in the goal-setting process, keep the following in mind:

Do
1. Decide which goals are most important.
2. Choose an easy one.
3. Decide what steps you are going to take to reach the goals.
4. Choose a positive person to discuss your goals with.
5. Set aside specific time to work on your goals.

Don't
1. Set goals that others think you should have.
2. Be in a hurry to select your goal.
3. Set very hard goals for yourself.

So, just suppose a miracle happened? And remember, little is good!

13

Coping with the Holidays

Holidays, and the anticipation of them, are extremely hard for a grieving person to cope with. When the word "holidays" is mentioned, most people think of Christmas. However, other special days can cause pain for those in grief, and each is very difficult to get through. For me (Kathy) those special days included not only Christmas but New Year's, Valentine's Day, Jerry's birthday, Easter, my birthday, Independence Day, our kids' birthdays, and Thanksgiving.

The one I found most difficult to endure was Thanksgiving—the one holiday Jerry and I always made extra special. We both appreciated that this was a holiday without the stress of gift-buying. We always started the day by hosting a light breakfast for close friends. This would end by noon, and soon Jerry's mother and aunt would arrive, as would my cousin. Each year we would buy a huge jigsaw puzzle and set it up on a card table in a corner of the living room. Jerry and the kids would spend the entire afternoon, off and on, putting it together. Puzzles were beyond my comprehension, so this was an activity the kids got to share exclusively with their father. While putting the puzzle together, we would all watch the movie *Auntie Mame*. The first few Thanksgivings after Jerry's death became a real challenge for us. By then, the close friends Jerry and I shared had all moved on. Jerry's mother opted to spend the day with her daughter, and we abandoned the ritual of the jigsaw puzzle and *Auntie Mame*. We had to create new rituals. This was very hard to do at first.

Memorial Day and Labor Day weekends—the beginning and end of camping season—are particularly hard for bereaved people who are campers. These are just a couple of difficult holidays other than Christmas.

The grieving person needs to equip himself to meet these challenging days. One thing you can do is to start a regular exercise program. Engaging in exercise will lift your spirits. Please note, we do not mean that exercise will make you happy. It will merely lift your spirits enough to see you through the day. Exercise will get you in physical shape.

The next thing you can do is to develop your faith. Everything seems to have been taken away, but your faith is always there, waiting to comfort you. At first it may not bring comfort at all, but ultimately it will, if you work at it. Developing your faith will get you in spiritual shape.

The third thing you can do is to journal. Start by writing the story of your relationship with the deceased, from the day it started right up to the present. It is amazing what will come out of that pen. It will be the best counseling you have ever had. With journaling, you start writing about one topic, but end immersed in a totally different one. It is really excellent therapy. Writing will get you in mental shape.

The fourth and final thing you can do is to start reading. When I married Jerry, I went from being Daddy's little girl to Jerry's little wife. After 24 years with Jerry, I didn't have a clue as to what my own opinion was on so many topics. My opinions had been meshed with Jerry's for so many years.

I knew I had to start developing as my own person, so I started reading self-help books. Before I knew it I had read 50 of them. That does *not* mean that I am neurotic. I prefer to look at it as being dedicated to good mental health. Besides, the weird part is not that I read 50 self-help books but that I *saw* myself in each one.

Grief is the process of working through your pain, but it also helps redefine who you are and where you fit in life. These books helped me to do exactly that. They taught me to become proactive, i.e., to stop and think before speaking. They taught me to become assertive instead of aggressive. Aggressive says, "Do it my way," whereas assertive says, "I'm doing it this way, you do what you want." Most importantly, these books taught me to set small, reachable goals. Reading helped keep my intellect in shape.

By spending 15 minutes each on exercising, developing your faith, journaling, and reading daily, you will be spending one hour a day, seven hours a week, twenty-eight hours a month building yourself up. Grief counselors always talk about "doing your grief work." These activities are the work they are talking about. Doing these four things will help you strengthen your mind, soul, and body, so you're better equipped to face the holidays.

Christmas is probably the toughest holiday for many people because it lasts so long. Christmas advertising starts in early October and continues until New Year's. That is three very long months of being accosted with memories that are bittersweet at best. There's no escaping the fact that this holiday is going to be difficult.

Take Christmas carols, for example. Some of them are so heart-wrenching, and most all of them carry memories, ones that literally span decades of your life! One of the hardest Christmas carols to listen to has to be "Have Yourself a Merry Little Christmas." The words are so significant: "Through the years, we all will be together, if the fates allow." Well, son of a gun, guess the fates didn't allow for those of us in grief, did they? So what do we do about these carols? A person who has never been in grief would probably say, "Turn them off, don't listen to them." This is great advice, except—where is the off switch in the grocery store, at the mall, or in the parking lot? Everywhere you go, it seems carols are playing. There's only one answer: prepare yourself to hear them. By preparing yourself, you may be able to tune them out.

Holiday shopping is the next thing you need to think about. Perhaps all those catalogs you receive in the mail will finally come in handy. Shopping by catalog eliminates having to fight crowds and make hasty decisions about what to buy. And many catalogs will deliver very close to Christmas. Another alternative to shopping is to give money as a gift. It's always the right color, and it never needs to be exchanged for a better fit.

If you do decide to venture out to the mall, however, don't make unrealistic demands on yourself. This is probably not the time to plan a shopping marathon. Remember how the grief cycle works. You might be having a good morning (positive response), but by afternoon you might be angry (negative response) or really depressed (agony phase). If you're having a good morning, by all means go shopping, but don't assume this mood will last all day. And don't be disappointed in yourself if you find you have to go home earlier than anticipated.

If a friend goes shopping with you, make it clear that you might have to cut the trip short. Remember, a friend will understand. However, try to avoid what happened to our friend Kim. She told her friend that she might not be able to stay at the mall too long. Her friend was very sympathetic, and about every ten minutes, she would ask, "Are you OK?" Kim was actually having a pretty good time, so this caring question was just a reminder of her grief. By all means prepare your friend, *but* tell him that *you* will let *him* know if you need to leave.

Everyone seems to have parties at holiday time, and this year you might get more invitations then ever before. Our advice is to accept each invitation you receive, *but* qualify your acceptance with, "If I can, I will." Also, drive yourself to the party. That way if you get there and just cannot bear to stay, you can leave without having to ask someone to take you home.

You will probably also get lots of Christmas cards. To send or not to send cards—that is the question. It's hard to pick an appropriate card. Most are filled with such happy thoughts, and you are decidedly not feeling that way this year. So what do you do? If you're a woman, you're going to have to deal with this issue or the guilt will probably overwhelm you. You know what they say—"Show me a woman who doesn't feel guilt and I'll show you a man." One solution is to send New Year's cards or write a brief note on holiday stationery. You can purchase New Year's cards after Christmas, *and* they will be on sale!

The next dilemma is—what do you say in the card or the note? Try something like "Thank you for thinking of me and sending a card. I'm thinking of you and wishing you all the best for the coming year." In other words, you can make it short, and you don't have to discuss how you're doing.

Decorating may be the last thing you feel like doing, but if you have children in the family, you may feel you have to. We both let our kids take care of it the first couple of years. My (Kathy's) eleven-year-old son thought it was great that he got to be in charge of arranging the decorations. He had a ball, and I didn't have to do a thing except admire his work.

From decorating, we move on to traditions and rituals of the holiday season. Rituals provide comfort under normal circumstances, but after the death, you may not feel you can relate to them in quite the same way. The first thing you need to do as you assess traditions is decide—is it really a tradition, or is it just a rut dressed up? If it is a tradition, it has played a part in your life for a long time, so serious consideration should be given it. Ask yourself—are you comfortable with it? Does it still hold positive meaning for you?

Sometimes traditions make very little sense. They are little more than something we engage in year after year without thinking. For example, there was a woman who was baking a ham for Christmas dinner. As her daughter stood watching, she saw her mother cut off each end of the ham. She asked the reason for doing that. Her mother replied that this was the way her mother had always done it. So the girl called her grandmother and was told, "That's the way my mother did it." She then decided to approach her great-grandmother about it, and the answer she got was, "It was during the Depression. The ham was big, the pan was small, so I cut off both ends of it so it would fit in the pan." This is a perfect example of a tradition that really doesn't have to be continued.

You also need to communicate your concerns to other family members. If there's a tradition that you really don't feel you can face, you may find out by communicating with others that they don't want to face it either.

This year it might seem like your loved one is with you more than you ever would have believed was possible. When my daughter Rachel got married, it seemed that everywhere I looked that day, I kept expecting to see her father. He was so much in my thoughts. With that in mind, the following is a good activity to honor your loved one's memory: You can create a treasure box.

Get a box from the grocery store and decorate it. Ask each person who spends the holidays with you to write down two or three special memories concerning the deceased. Without sharing these remembrances, yet, place them in the box. Next, have each person select a keepsake they have from the deceased and place it in the box. Again, don't share what makes that keepsake special, yet. Last, have each person write down one or two funny memories about the deceased, and put those in the box, too, without sharing them yet. If small children are involved in this activity, they can draw pictures of their memories and place them in the box too. Designate a time during the holiday festivities to gather around the box. One by one, each person removes the items he placed in the box, reads outloud what he wrote, and shares the significance of the keepsake.

Read the funny memories last, so the activity ends with laughter. You can use it as a celebration of your loved one's life. It can also be a stepping stone to better communication. Someone will surely bring up a long-forgotten memory, and this will lead to other memories. This is such a life-ministering activity to engage in, and yields such positive results.

When a friend's father died, I (Kathy) waited a month and then sent her a card. I reminisced about how funny her dad was. I wrote about his "advice" to the grandchildren when they were young. He would tell them, "Don't play with your food, and if it's not a toy, don't touch it." When I saw her soon after she received my card, she told me that her family had totally forgotten that her dad used to say those "words of wisdom" to the kids. My card brought back other funny remembrances about her father, and it really helped them to lift the burden of grief for just a brief time.

The most important thing to remember about the holidays is that they are stressful for everyone. It just seems more so to you this year. You probably always felt somewhat stressed at holiday time, trying to get everything done right. With that in mind, be kind to yourself, indulge yourself, and be understanding of yourself. You're in grief!

14

Tension Units

Working your way through the grief cycle, trying to help a child deal with the loss of a loved one, or coping with the holidays can all be complicated by what Jack Canfield calls "tension units."[9] We are created to be fulfilled and complete. When a death occurs, our life is suddenly lacking and imperfect. It doesn't matter if the death was sudden or anticipated, we just feel incomplete. Our goals and dreams have been thwarted, and the tension builds.

We have to get rid of this tension, or it can cause both emotional and physical problems. We are made to carry only so much tension, and when we are in grief, we are probably overloaded with it. We lack emotional as well as physical strength, so we can't think clearly or take care of even the most mundane chores. We know that things need doing, but we just don't have the strength. So the tension units build.

When I (Kathy) had been in grief for about a year, I took a stress inventory test, which measured the stress in my life. The test consisted of a list of 43 "Life Events." Each event had a number value. I was supposed to review the list and circle any of the events that were relevant to me. They ranged from death of a spouse, with a number value of 100, to a minor violation of the law, with a number value of only 11. After reviewing it, I tallied my score and found it totaled 630 points.

A person with a normal amount of stress in their life will score 150–200 points. A score of 300 indicates major stress. Since I had more than double that score, I probably should have been dead by this point. Yet, here I was. As odd as this may sound, that test really encouraged me. Even with this incredible burden of stress on me, I was still functioning. I wasn't functioning well, but I was functioning nevertheless. It was also very obvious that I had to reduce some of this stress before it did major damage.

An easy way to understand tension units is to visualize your head encased by many key hooks. You are only made to carry so much weight on each key hook, and this weight needs to constantly be redistributed. If all the key hooks are filled to capacity, you're on overload.

To start unloading the tension units, you can use Canfield's "do, delegate or dump" method.[10] Look at an unfinished project and do it (finish it), delegate it (give it to someone else to do), or dump it (abandon it). As you choose to do one of these things, you'll automatically feel somewhat better. First of all, you will have made a decision to take action. Secondly, you will have recognized the tension unit for what it is and taken a positive step to deal with it.

I (Mark) hired a cleaning lady after Sherry died. I was able to come home to a clean house, and it felt great. I also switched to perennials in the yard, and was free the following spring from unwanted, complicated yard work. Do anything that will help you get free from tension. It will give you a feeling of control over your life.

Do, delegate, or dump is a refreshing concept. Don't feel guilty if you choose to dump a task rather than do it. You may feel obligated to complete it, but if it has remained undone for a long period of time, it obviously wasn't all that important. So take the plunge—dump it!

When you finally decide to get rid of a tension unit in your life, it is cause for celebration. Congratulate yourself. If you finally accomplish a task you were not up to completing before, or make it through a portion of the day without crying, cursing, or feeling depressed, walk around the room with clenched fists and shout, "I did it, I accomplished it, I overcame."

Attempt at least twice a day to sense the emotional freedom you are feeling due to the elimination of a tension unit. After all, what you continually search for is what you will ultimately find. And, what you ultimately are searching for is complete healing as you work your way through the grief cycle. When you sense this emotional freedom, you will feel stronger. The proverb "Sleep is sweet to the working man" refers not only to physical labor but mental labor as well. When you have eliminated tension units from your life, you will be able to rest much better—and rest is such an important ingredient for a healthy life.

When better rested, you can become more of a participant in life. Your self-image will be enhanced. You will feel more resilient, creative in your work, and ambitious. All this adds up to improved self-esteem. This enhanced self-image will also help fight off depression, anger, and guilt, which can have such a detrimental effect on your well-being. It can be used as a weapon to combat the ugly feelings that can engulf you when you are in the negative response phase of the grief cycle.

Becoming more active is a real challenge when you're in grief. It is often the last thing you want to do. How can you possibly feel motivated to be more active when you can barely get out of your chair? I (Kathy) would sit for what seemed like hours at a time, not having the strength to do anything but cry. I remember Rachel telling me three weeks after Jerry's death that we had to go to the store because we had no food. I told her to fix a sandwich. She then told me we didn't have any crackers, bread, or anything else. The cupboards were literally bare. When I finally managed to get up from my chair, I was amazed to discover that she wasn't exaggerating. We literally had no food left. I was so preoccupied with my grief that I didn't see our groceries dwindling to nothing.

I also couldn't sleep for more than three hours at night. I would wake up at 4 every morning. By 5:30, I could lie in bed no longer. The problem was that there was nothing to do at 5:30 in the morning. The only place open was the gym. Finally one morning I just had to get out of the house, so I drove there. I began exercising and actually came home feeling that I could face the day ahead—well, the morning anyway.

Exercise had released endorphins throughout my mind and body. Endorphins are chemicals in your brain that give you a psycho-physical lift and a sense of well-being. They are released through motion, so they're always available to you. By exercising, you will get those endorphins pumping throughout your system, and they'll help improve your mood. If you're not exercising, give it a try. You might be surprised at how much better you will feel. If you can begin to exercise regularly, you'll feel more like getting actively involved in life again.

15

Neural Passages

When you are in the first phase of the grief cycle, in shock, you are numb. Your mind is not made to compute such horrific information all at once, so it must do so a little at a time. You are stunned; you still hope things will go back to normal and your loved one will come back. This is a normal abnormality.

I (Kathy) spent the first few days after Jerry died trying to think of how to bring him back to life. In my saner moments, I knew this was impossible, but I found myself trying anyway. I would wake up in the morning and be sure—for just an instant—that it had all been a bad dream, but then reality would set in. I would be forced once again to confront the knowledge that he was dead.

If this happens to you, it is because your loved one is still literally alive in your head. If you were to open up a person's skull and examine the brain, you would find that it is made up of neural fibers that come to life during a thought. Each time the same thought occurs, the same neural fiber is used. This neural fiber then becomes a neural pathway, meaning the thought is now common and established in the brain. When the pathway continues to be used over and over, it becomes a neural highway. When the neural highways are used continually, they become like superhighways.

We use the term neural superhighway because the thought pattern is so embedded in your brain that you respond in certain familiar situations without thinking. The neural highway has been activated, and you don't have to think it through. The thought process in these particular situations has become automatic.

For example, if you are driving down a familiar road and realize you have navigated a block or a mile without consciously perceiving it, you were able to do so because your neural highway was functioning. You were responding without conscious thought.

If this can happen while driving a familiar street, how much more does it occur in situations concerning your loved one? Stop and think for a moment about all the thoughts you've had each day, week, month, and year concerning your loved one since he or she came into your life. Your mind is biologically constructed to handle those millions of thoughts of your loved one. These thoughts establish pathways, highways, and superhighways. This means that this person is physically in your brain. If a surgeon touched one of these neural fibers, you would think in all reality that you were experiencing your loved one again. When the mind's electricity surges through these neural fibers, it reproduces the thoughts and experiences of your loved one. These neural fibers are constructed to receive and release electricity that moves through them in order to respond to life situations.

For as long as you have been together, your neural fibers have been conditioned to relate to your loved one. After a loss, there are often moments, or perhaps longer periods, when time is blocked out. You may not remember how that time was passed. This is because your mind's electricity has created an overload in your neural fibers. Those thoughts of your loved one had nowhere to go, so your brain, for lack of a better term, short-circuited.

It takes years for these neural highways to shrink, and they will never disappear completely. They will only dwindle as your loved one's freshness and reality subsides. New thoughts will replace old neural fibers and those powerful memories that created the grieving experience.

When doctors, ministers, or others in caring professions make statements like, "You must get yourself together, you must move on" or "Forgive so you can heal and move on," they're showing that they don't understand how complicated the mind's structure is. There's no way you can instantly forgive or quickly heal, because the mind takes years to reduce the powerful neural passages that have been created in the brain. It would be better for them to say nothing than to give such unenlightened advice.

Anthony Robbins describes the neural pathway concept in _Awaken the Giant Within._ He writes about a scientist named Merzenich who did research involving a monkey's brain. Merzenich trained a monkey to move his finger in order to earn his food. He then "remapped the touch-activated areas in the monkey's brain. He found that the area responding to the signals from that finger's additional use had expanded in size nearly 600 percent."[10] Merzenich then trained the monkey to respond a different way in order to receive food. After using this new response for a measured period of time, he discovered that new neural pathways had been created. "The good news is this: research has also shown that when the monkey was forced to stop using his finger, the area of the brain where these neuro connections were made actually began to shrink in size, and therefore the neuro-association weakened."[11]

This should be an encouragement to you who are constantly thinking of a lost loved one. All of those bombarding, painful thoughts will slowly diminish over time. The neural highways will shrink to neural pathways, and the overpowering pain associated with them will decrease. Your brain has the marvelous ability to reclaim these memories at will, but eventually, when reclaimed, they will be free from the pain you are feeling now. Knowing your brain has this capability helps explain why different incidents trigger memories of your loved one. He or she is always going to be a part of you.

When I (Kathy) found out several years after Jerry's death that one of our favorite restaurants was closing permanently, it immediately brought to mind many good memories that I hadn't thought of in a long time. The neural highways concerning them had definitely shrunk, but they came alive again instantly upon hearing that news. Enough time had passed, however, and I was able to recall those memories with a fondness that was free of pain. You can take comfort and be encouraged that the memories of your loved one will never be lost, but the pain of them will lessen over time. They will eventually become bittersweet and finally, just sweet.

16

Forgiveness

I (Kathy) grew very bitter after Jerry died, because people I thought I could count on didn't seem to be there for me. This was another loss to mourn, a secondary loss. This left me feeling confused and furthered my inability to cope. Dr. Rosalyn Karaban, a professor at St. Bernard's Seminary, who lost a loved one to death, said, "I now look at the world through the eyes of death."[12] Death not only robs you of your loved one, but of healthy perceptions about life as well.

We are all born with three basic needs: to be accepted, to have value, and to attain worthiness. Before the death I had been Super Mom—Brownie leader, Girl Scout leader, Cub Scout leader, softball coach. It all stopped when Jerry died—all of it! Those articles and advertisements that portray warm family scenes used to reflect my life—college sweethearts, still in love after 19 years of marriage, more in love with each passing year, etc, etc. We were a walking cliché, and then suddenly it was over! The one who had accepted me unconditionally, made me feel of worth, and valued what I accomplished as both his wife and the mother of his children was gone. I no longer felt accepted, worthy or valued. I no longer had a sense of trust. I was too aware that everything I valued could be taken away instantly. My future was now clouded by the pain of what had happened to me.

Before the death, I was a very optimistic person. I now found myself becoming angry, cynical, and resentful at the least provocation. I began to feel rejected by people, though in reality, I was pushing them away. I developed an "I don't care" attitude. My anger was very hard to cope with, as was being suspicious and depressed so much of the time. Scripture says that if we don't forgive, we are turned over to the tormentors. I was definitely feeling tormented, so I knew what I had to do: I had to forgive so I could finally reclaim my acceptance, worthiness, and value. The first step toward doing this was to forgive those I thought had wronged me. Next I had to forgive myself for things I had said and done.

Often after a death, the survivor needs to find the fortitude to forgive. Sometimes he needs to forgive the one who died, and he may need to forgive God as well for allowing it to happen. Forgiveness is one of the most powerful tools available to us. To discover whether there is a forgiveness issue in your life, ask yourself three questions: Are you at peace with God? Are you at peace with others? And, are you at peace with yourself? If not, you need to forgive.

Lewis Smedes writes in *The Art of Forgiving* that when we forgive, we heal our minds. Forgiving was the only way to be fair to myself, to make it possible to be suspicion-free and optimistic once again. Forgiving was probably the best gift I ever gave myself. Many others benefited, too, because I became easier to be around. I no longer looked for a person's "hidden agenda." The person who benefited most, however, was me.

Forgiveness is voluntary. No one can make another forgive. There will come a time when you find the strength to deal with any forgiveness issues. Sometimes the person you're forgiving might not even know he needs forgiveness. He might have hurt you unintentionally, and you may have said nothing at the time. In this case, you should forgive him without trying to explain the problem. Consider it now behind you and move on. When you forgive, you set both the person and yourself free. You will feel as if a burden has been lifted from you. For the most part, your "demons" will have vanished.

You are only human, though, and because you may have had unforgiving thoughts toward the person for quite a while, you might find yourself replaying some of those thoughts from time to time. If that happens, stop and remind yourself that you forgave the person and you don't need to think about it anymore. This might be hard to do at first, because you've developed deep neural passages concerning the unforgiveness, but with practice it can be accomplished.

When you have truly achieved this, you will be in control of your emotions once again. They will no longer dominate you in negative ways. You'll be able to step back, assess situations, and respond appropriately. You'll get to choose the emotional outcomes in your life. Your heart will not be bogged down with "issues." Antonio Porchia says, "In a full heart, there is room for everything but in an empty heart, there is room for nothing."

I (Kathy) was able to do a lot of forgiving when I could see that much of what I was looking at "through the eyes of death" was misperception on my part. I felt rejected, so

121

I had built walls around me. Before I made the decision to forgive, I would have insisted that these walls were there as protection. But after forgiveness took place, I saw that they were really walls that confined me and kept me from progressing.

There is a story about an escape artist who was very successful at escaping from any confinement. He was finally foiled in his attempt to escape from an old, rustic jail cell. When he at last gave up, the sheriff walked in and opened the door without turning the key in the lock. The escape artist had been tricked into thinking that the door was locked. He had never checked, and had spent hours needlessly devising intricate ways to escape. When you need to forgive, you may wrestle for hours with your own unlocked doors. Forgiveness opens that door, and you can walk out free any time.

17

Dreams

Albert Einstein attributed his theory of relativity to a dream. Both the Old and New Testaments describe dreams: dreams from God to believers, unbelievers, saints, and sinners. All were given dreams to establish and develop both His will and their destiny. In *A Psychological View of Conscience,* Carl Jung writes: "There is no question that dreams come from a wisdom beyond our own. Dreams can help us determine who we are and what we are becoming. They can be especially helpful to the person in grief."[13]

In dreams, the supernatural can do its work. In sleep, your soul is freer and less analytical, so you're more open to creative understanding and development. The essential nature of dreams is personal, and you must understand them in terms of your own life. Dreams can be seen as revelations and guidance.

If you look at dreams as a positive, creative force, your conscious mind will accept what the subconscious is attempting to reveal. The basic premise to understanding dreams is that they are almost always symbolic. For example, a house represents your person. If you dream of a kitchen, that is where your creativity takes place. An attic represents your thought life while a basement represents the deep, hidden issues of your life. Dreams about transportation—cars, boats, trains, buses—are really about an emotional journey or development. Fearful things like being chased by people or animals (alligators, bears, lions, etc.) can be interpreted as dreams about strong emotional qualities that you need to accept. Dreams about a snake could mean that you are shedding something from your life, just as the snake sheds its skin. Perhaps new concepts are being developed in your life. Talking on the telephone in a dream usually means you are getting a wake-up call about something you need to resolve.

Dreams of male/female issues generally represent the male/female emotional sides of the psyche, as all people have both a male and a female side. When you dream about someone you know, the dream is not about that person, but about that person's most prevalent quality or characteristic. So when you dream of someone, ask yourself what he represents to you. If you decide, for example, that he represents integrity, then integrity is probably the issue your subconscious is working on.

I (Mark) was talking with a friend named Scholar, and he told me about a recurring dream he had been having. He was walking up a steep bridge with railings. At the top of the bridge there were no railings and he felt threatened. I asked him if he had been having the dream for the last four or five years, knowing he had recently retired. He told me yes, that was about when the dream had started. I asked him if he thought he was subconsciously concerned about retirement. Before retirement there was security (the bridge railing), but having left his occupational years behind, he might now feel threatened; the top of the bridge with no rails could represent a threat to safety. He said, "That's it!" He was delighted to finally be able to figure out what it all had meant.

How do you know which interpretation of a dream is the right one? You'll react the way Scholar did when you hear it. Your dreams are personal, and they're always meant strictly for you. If someone has to convince you of the meaning, then it's incorrect.

I (Kathy) had an dream that was both amusing and informative. I was in my house and the phone rang (wake-up call). A friend of mine was calling to tell me that I should have sent her mother a Christmas card. She was yelling at me, and all of a sudden my door opened and she walked into my house, still talking to me on her cell phone. When she saw me, she stopped, pointed at me, and yelled, "The trouble with you is that you are inflexible." When I woke up and began to analyze the dream's meaning, I thought of the big issues in my life at that time. Rachel was going to be married soon and I knew my relationship with her would have to change. The interpretation I made was this: the most prevalent characteristic of the woman who called me on the phone was that she is very inflexible. Since that was also what she had called me, I knew that inflexibility was the issue my subconscious was working on. The meaning of the dream became clear immediately. It was a wake-up call telling me that I had to become more flexible where Rachel was concerned.

Dreams have inspired people since the dawn of mankind. In the early years of Christianity, the Church employed professional dream interpreters. They knew the value of dreams and understood them to be not only psychologically sound but spiritually directed. They considered dream interpretation necessary for a person's complete development.

An excellent and simple book to read to understand dreamwork and dream interpretation is *The Encyclopedia of Dreams* by Rosemary Guiley. Perceiving the true meaning of dreams can be of great help while your conscious is emotionally healing and your subconscious is attempting to show you where you truly are in the recovery process of the grief cycle.

18

Give Yourself a Break!

Your ability to survive the intense pain of losing a loved one is a tribute to your inner fortitude. Most of the time, however, you probably don't see it that way at all. You reprimand yourself frequently because you think you should be better able to cope with your grief. As you work your way through the grief cycle, you have to accept the reality that there is no such thing as perfect grieving. Perfectionism and grief just don't mix. In fact, if you tried to be perfect when you grieved, it would just add to the burden you are already carrying.

If you grieved perfectly, you wouldn't miss your loved one, because you would have your memories to sustain you. They would be all you needed to get you through the grief. You would look forward to holidays and anniversaries, because that is when you would allow yourself to relive all the memories of your loved one. That would be a fulfilling and sustaining experience. You would have no concentration problems, nor would the grief interfere with your daily life. You would devise a new schedule to live by quite soon after the funeral. This would make perfect sense, because why live in the past?

You would think of the death only once in a while. After all, there's nothing you could do about it, so it would be pointless to dwell on it. You would work your way through grief in a logical way, since that would be the only way to really do it right. You would look forward to each day and anticipate the future with a positive attitude. After a year or so, you would be pretty much over the grief. You would finally be able to put it behind you and move on.

In other situations we encounter, some of the above might be good advice, but it just doesn't work for someone in grief. Our thoughts influence our feelings, and at no other time in our lives have our thoughts and feelings been so intense. We cannot help but meditate on what has happened to us; otherwise, how do we make sense of it?

It is vital to understand that our thoughts not only influence our feelings but also our physical and social well-being. I (Mark) attended two seminars, one at The Family Therapy Institute, sponsored by the University of Rochester, and the other, "Spirituality & Healing in Medicine," sponsored by Harvard Medical School. They both attested to the bio-psycho-spiritual-social model of illness and wellness. I learned how a person's spiritual and emotional makeup affects his physical health, which consequently influences his interactions with people. If one area is affected, all four areas will be affected. This is true to such an extent that the University of Rochester statistics show that only 13 percent of the people in hospitals are there because of an illness that originated biologically. The others are there because of an internal problem that affected them both emotionally and physically. Hence, their interpersonal relationships were also damaged. If you have an emotional problem that you cannot resolve, it will eventually become a physical problem. When this happens, it cannot help but influence your relationships.

During one of these seminars, one of the participants saw the truth of what we were learning. He always knew he had unresolved emotional issues with his father. What he never realized until taking this seminar, however, was that these issues had far-reaching consequences. He learned how they had negatively affected his two previous marriages, as well as his present one. This was a revelation to him, and he decided that upon returning home he would get professional counseling to finally work out his issues in hopes of saving his presently troubled marriage.

If a particular grief issue is a stumbling block for you, then as soon as you have the strength, find a way to work on it and release it. Some of these stumbling blocks might include anger, depression, bitterness, isolation, or loneliness. The first step toward resolving the issue is to honestly identify what it is and admit how it is causing you to stumble in your relationships. Look for ways to rid yourself of it. Perhaps you could seek professional help. Possibly you could find a good friend with a listening ear. If you are fortunate to find this good friend, be honest with him about the problem and the extent of it. Search until you find the emotional answer before it becomes a physical problem. Otherwise, you can be complicating your grief journey.

A good way to determine if you have a stumbling block is to look at your relationships. Do people tend to move toward you or away from you? Do you have close friends or just acquaintances? If people tend to move away from you, and your life is peopled more with acquaintances than close friends, you can probably assume you have a stumbling block that needs attention. We are social animals. A well-rounded, fulfilling life includes healthy, personal relationships.

If you have no complicated grief issues, there will come a time when you will once again have control over your emotions and your thoughts. Your emotions will be something you can choose to experience, or not. They will be a tool for you to use. They will not be a crutch to lean on or to blame for your bad reactions to things. You will not use them to keep people away. You will discover that your thoughts are healthy again. You will also find that instead of your emotions controlling your thoughts, your thoughts are now controlling your emotions.

19

Hope

Hope is something we are born with. It is the innocence of expecting life to be fair and rewarding. Everyone has hope, and we grow and change according to how much hope we have. When we experience the death of a loved one, our hope is temporarily destroyed and we stop growing for a time. In his book *Death and Grief: A Guide for the Clergy,* Alan Woefelt writes: "Grief is an experience of many losses—the loss of self, ideas, dreams, and faith."[14]

Though it cannot be seen much, the one thing that usually persists through the four phases of grief is hope. During the shock, hope is there. It is the hope that this is not real, that this is a test. You believe in your heart that it will go away, that you will wake up and find you've had a bad dream and your loved one is still with you. During the agony, hope is there. It is the hope that this hurt will stop and there will be life again. During the negative response, hope is there too. It is the hope that this darkness, which you don't understand and which brings anger, depression, and loneliness, will disappear. It is hope that finally brings you to the fourth and final phase of grief: the positive response. In this phase you finally regain the ability to experience the hope that has long been hidden in the first three phases.

Elizabeth Kubler-Ross, who has produced some of the most fruitful work concerning people who are dying, writes that she "found that all our patients maintained a little bit of it (hope) and were nurtured by it in especially difficult times."[15] This is proof that hope is always there, even in the most seemingly hopeless situations. Depending on where you are in the grief cycle, flickers of hope could be just starting to appear momentarily again. When this happens, you will soon start to see this hope for more sustained periods of time.

Samuel Coleridge wrote that "hope without an object cannot live." At this point in your life, you have to search for what is going to give you the hope to live. There are different avenues you can take in your search. Some avenues will be philosophical, some relational, and some religious. People who have successfully been on this search minimize the negatives they encounter, embrace problem-solving, and can laugh at themselves. They also have friends to share the journey with. They use prayer and/or meditation to restore their inner strength. They exercise and try their best to stay healthy. They focus on their goals. All of this helps them to find hope and keep it alive.

You should embrace your grief; it will make you healthy. It is your friend, but don't make it your ugly friend. Don't wear it like a badge of honor. Don't be the type of person who always seems to be saying things like, "Look at me, my spouse died." Be careful not to use your grief as your only source of significance.

As Erma Mae Perkins, a nurse/educator for Hospice, writes in *The Final Ascent*, a grief journey is like scaling a mountain. A traveler to the summit of a mountain can choose many different paths to follow. He can travel with companions or go it alone. He must equip himself with different tools, and will do so according to his personal needs. The climber discards more and more items as he approaches the summit, because the air gets thin. He gets tired and can no longer bear up under the weight of his equipment. As he nears the end of his ascent, he gains the understanding that now he must crest this mountain alone. It has become an individual journey, because his internal fortitude and willpower are required to succeed.

On your grief journey, you're traveling up the mountain of life. You're making the journey alone, although, we hope, with much support. Instead of starting with tools, you start with emotional baggage. As the journey progresses toward emotional healing, you discard much of this baggage, just as the climber discards the weight of his no-longer-needed tools. Finally, you choose to be unburdened from the weight of grief. Now you can reach the summit, and see that you can live again. Whereas the mountain climber begins the journey with strength and ends exhausted, you begin exhausted but end with strength.

One way to regain this strength is to join a bereavement support group. Many people find it very helpful to be with others who are struggling to deal with the same multitude of feelings. A support group can give you needed guidance and empathy. Hospice is an excellent organization to contact for help in finding the right group. Often, support group members will confess that prior to their loss, they didn't think of themselves as the type who would join a group like this. But they finally had to admit that they needed the strength of others to help them regain their own strength.

Sometimes the bereaved person's newfound strength can display itself in seemingly odd ways. Having been raised in

Missouri, a goal I (Mark) always had from the time I was a boy was to ride a Brahma bull in a rodeo. As I grew up and adult responsibilities took over, I shelved this childhood fantasy. But after the death of Sherry, when I was 42 years old, the opportunity presented itself and I thought, *Why not?* People who knew me, however, thought, *Why?*

While preparing to ride the bull I had the distinct impression that THIS is what life should be about—breaking out of a mundane existence and trying something totally beyond one's control. It is something one must do alone. Friends and spectators were quick to cheer me on in this endeavor, but they were only observers.

When the cowboys were strapping me onto the bull, the sights, sounds, and smells all confirmed that something new was about to happen. The excitement I felt was reinforced when I was finally strapped to the bull and told to put my tailbone on his backbone without putting much weight on it. When I did, I watched the bull's muscles expand in all directions at once. While my amazement was also expanding, the bull collapsed in the pen. I was pulled head-long down into the chute with my boots still caught in the wooden barriers overhead. I remember thinking, *I'm hugging a bull upside down.*

The cowboys were standing above me, shouting down to me, "Spur him!" I uprighted myself as much as I could, while still being strapped on, and asked if that was what I should really do. They replied with a resounding, "Yes, spur the bull," as they fled from their safe perches. So I spurred the bull!

I only thought I was prepared for the ride I got, as the bull reared up on his hind legs and attempted to vault over the chute wall. I was amazed at how my mind could tabulate so much information at one time. I was trying to hold on and at the same time let go. I could hear the crowd cheering and the cowboys yelling something. I felt the pressure on my legs caught between the boards, knowing that I could be crushed. I was thinking, *A black and white bull, I can do it.*

After calming the bull down, I could hear the cowboys off in the distance instructing me about something. What I could hear most vividly, however, was the blood pumping in my head as the adrenaline screamed throughout my body. As I focused on reality, I saw a huge red nose looking at me, and behind it, a clown telling me to listen to them. A cowboy was saying, "Nod your head, and we'll open the gate."

I didn't want to nod my head! I knew what was going to happen if I did. But you only go around once, so I nodded my head. The gate opened, the bull and I exited, and suddenly that bull was going anywhere he wanted to go. All I remember is listening to tremendous jarring and snapping noises as well as the sound of hoofbeats. Oh yes, you can hear hoofbeats while you're falling off a bull. They sound like shovels digging into the ground, right beside your head.

I do not remember much of the ride or the fall off the bull. It was probably best summed up in the question of a young boy from our church who asked his mother, "Why did Pastor Ammerman go 'oof'?" The ride lasted six seconds, and I dislocated my wrist.

As I stood muddleheaded in the ring, the announcer asked me how the ride was. The clown was yelling at me to watch out for the bull, the crowd was cheering, and I was looking at my hat on the ground and thinking, *My new cowboy hat is dirty.* I picked it up as the clown reached me and guided me out of the bull's way. I shouted to the announcer, "It was great," and I left the arena to the applause of the crowd.

That is what I've found life to be like. Most people will be only spectators at best, never desiring nor understanding the thrill of the challenge. Some will ridicule and jeer. Others will be content to help, but stay on the sidelines. This is fine; each person is needed to make society complete. But wholeness comes with challenge. It requires us to expand our horizons, to shake off the limitations that have been placed on us by circumstances or catastrophes beyond our control. Living life is taking the challenge to be whole in our spirit, soul, and body. To be overcomers, courageous and healed is a choice.

So, come on. You can do it! Ride the bull!

Endnotes

1. Norman Cousins. *The Healing Heart* (New York: Avon Books, 1983), 64.
2. Doug Manning. *Don't Take My Grief Away* (New York: Harper/Row, 1984), 66.
3. Susan McClelland. *If There's Anything I Can Do* (Gainesville: Triad, 1990), 68.
4. Carol Straudacher. *Beyond Grief* (Oakland: New Harbinger, 1987), 72.
5. Alan Woefelt. *Death and Grief: A Guide for the Clergy* (Bristol: Accelerated Development, 1988), 74.
6. Karen Gravelle. *Teenagers Face to Face with Bereavement* (Englewood Cliffs: Silver Burdett, 1989), 81.
7. Ibid., 81.
8. Claudia Jewitt. *Helping Children Cope with Separation and Loss* (Harvard: Harvard Commons, 1982), 84.
9. Jack Canfield. *How to Build High Self-Esteem* (Conant Niles: Nightingale, 1993), 103.
10. Anthony Robbins. *Awaken the Giant Within* (New York: Fireside, 1991), 110.
11. Ibid., 110.

12. Carl Jung. *Dreams* (Princeton: Princeton University Press, 1974), 116.
13. Alan Woefelt. *Death and Grief: A Guide for the Clergy* (Bristol: Accelerated Development, 1988), 124.
14. Elizabeth Kubler-Ross. *On Death and Dying* (New York: Collier Books, 1969), 124.

Bibliography

Berg, Insoo Kim, *Interviewing for Solutions*. Pacific Grove: Brooks/Cole, 1998.

Branden, Nathaniel. *Honoring the Self*. New York: Bantam, 1986.

Canfield, Jack *How to Build High Self-Esteem*. Conant Niles: Nightingale, 1993.

Cousins, Norman. *The Healing Heart*. New York: Avon Books, 1983.

Fitzgerald, Helen. *The Grieving Child*. New York: Fireside, 1992.

Gee, Bobbi. *Winning the Image Game*. Berkeley: Page Mill, 1991.

Guiley, Rosemary. *The Encyclopedia of Dreams*. New York: Berkeley, 1995.

Gravelle, Karen. *Teenagers Face to Face with Bereavement*. Englewood Cliffs: Silver Burdett, 1989.

Jewitt, Claudia. *Helping Children Cope with Separation and Loss*. Harvard: Harvard Commons, 1982.

Jung, Carl. *Dreams*. Princeton: Princeton University Press, 1974.

Kubler-Ross, Elizabeth. *On Death and Dying*. New York: Collier Books, 1969.

Manning, Doug. *Don't Take My Grief Away*. New York: Harper/Row, 1984.

McClelland, Susan. *If There's Anything I Can Do*. Gainesville: Triad, 1990.

Perkins, Erma. *The Final Ascent*. Rochester Genesee Region Home Care, 1998.

Rando, Therese. *How to Go On Living When Someone You Love Dies*. New York: Bantam Books, 1991.

Robbins, Anthony. *Awaken the Giant Within*. New York: Fireside, 1991.

Smedes, Lewis. *The Art of Forgiving*. New York: Moorings, 1996.

Straudacher, Carol. *Beyond Grief*. Oakland: New Harbinger, 1987.

"What If I Grieved Perfectly?" *Bereavement Magazine*. May/June 1995.

Woefelt, Alan. *Death and Grief: A Guide for Clergy*. Bristol: Accelerated Development, 1988.

To order additional copies of

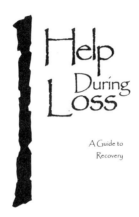

Help During Loss

A Guide to
Recovery

send $9.95 plus shipping and handling to

Books, Etc.
PO Box 4888
Seattle, WA 98104

or have your credit card ready and call

(800) 917-BOOK